Dear Pc

God Bless

Hope you enjoy

the Story.

Perry L. Montague

John 14: 1

PERRY T. MONTAGUE

Dedication

This book is respectfully dedicated to our veterans and their families who have sacrificed so much for America. There will never be enough words to fully express the appreciation they deserve for their bravery, patriotism and sacrifice.

"Greater Love has no one than this: To lay down one's life for one's friend." JOHN 15:13

Acknowledgements

$\mathcal{I}$ am so thankful for the life I have and it is my hope that the readers of The Treasures of Summerville will enjoy going to a place where life is simpler, full and rewarding. I pray you to will get a blessing when reading it as I leave it up to the reader to identify with the characters in their own way.

To all of the great friends who have allowed me to use their names and good character, I can only offer much heartfelt appreciation. To my patient family, especially my wife Lynn, I offer love and thanks as this has been a long road for you also. I also have to offer a very special thanks to five other great souls.

To Mark: You're honest never ending encouragement and friendship lifted me up so many times on this project. I consider myself blessed to have you as a friend.

To Joyce: Your sunny outlook on life is priceless and can only come from one source. Thank you for all of the stories and personalities of the characters from the past you shared with me, and for the support and honest input. I hope I did them justice.

To Doris: You were there for me when this project was just a random thought, and you have been encouraging me ever since. Your love and energy are matchless. I am thankful you are in my life.

To Debra Hooper (My Illustrator and Friend): A very special thanks to you as you have a rare God given talent to bring an idea to the canvas like no one I have ever seen. This project would never have been complete if you had not given your time and selfless talent. You have completed this story with your fantastic illustrations.

To my Uncle Lewis who experienced the worst part of World War II. I will be forever grateful for you lending me just a few of your war experiences but mostly for your service to America. (My Uncle was wounded three times in the war and is a Veteran of the Battle of the Bulge as well as many other campaigns.)

"THAT THE TRIAL OF YOUR FAITH, BEING MUCH MORE PRECIOUS THAN OF GOLD THAT PERISHETH, THOUGH IT BE TRIED WITH FIRE, MIGHT BE FOUND UNTO PRAISE AND HONOR AND GLORY AT THE APPEARING OF JESUS CHRIST."

I PETER 1:7

Table of Contents

The Town 23

Angela 27

Moving Back Home 30

Aunt Evelyn 33

The Surprise 36

The Tour 47

The Secret Room 57

Father and Son 61

The Stage Coach Robber 71

Questions 78

Memorial Hill 80

Bobi Stone 85

Monte and Sam 88

The Tree House 93

The Final Clue 96

Cousin Walton 99

The New Detector 103

The Business Trip 105

The Plan. 107

Run 111

That Sick Feeling 119

Fatherly Advice 124

The Decision 130

A Wise Teacher 132

Scared Stiff 137

The Visit. 144

Semper Fi 153

Sunday Evening 162

Organizing 169

Paint Up, Fix Up And Just Visiting. 173

Fall. 177

History 181

A Mystery Revealed. 183

Warm Holidays 199

Fil And Mil 202

A Christmas Eve To Remember 204

A Life Changing Message 216

Lit'l O's Knight 223

Winter Excitement 233

Is That What I Think It Is? 238

Searching The Barn. 243

The Family Bible 249

Spring Fever Or Gold Fever 258

Rattlesnake Bend 261

The Great Treasure Hunt. 266

More Hunting. 272

Impatience. 280

The Old Oak Stump 289

Jackpot 294

A Close Call. 297

A King's Ransom 304

Counting The Loot. 308

The Coin Collector 311

Unbelievable 316

The Secret Club. 327

All Aboard 345

A Prayer Answered 354

The Breakfast Meeting. 358

The Best Of The Best 366

A Worthy Project 373

Misty 377

A Passed Tragedy 382

A Present Tragedy. 398

Old Times 405

The Front Porch. 409

A Picnic To Remember 413

Ben's Legacy. 422

Happiness And Sorrow 425

John 14:1. 429

The Final Goodbye 438

Traveler 443

Catching Up With Things. 445

The Monument 449

Life Goes On 457

The Treasures of Summerville

By Perry T. Montague

Beep…Beep…Beep… BEEEEEEP.

"Hey Dad, whatcha think it is?"

"I don't know Christopher, but whatever it is, the detector is saying it is solid metal and it is about four to six inches deep."

"You think it could be GOLD?" Christopher asked anxiously.

"Could be, let's dig and find out." Paul answered.

"Here, take the digger and go at it, but be careful, we don't want to damage any treasure that's under there; you just never know what you'll find with "Old Betsy." Paul said.

"Old Betsy" was the nickname Christopher's father had given their metal detector. Why had he named it that, well, he just thought it sounded like a reliable name and it didn't hurt that it was the name of Davy Crockett's rifle and Davy Crockett was one of Paul Taylor's favorite historical figures from his home state of Tennessee. You could always count on Old Betsy to find something interesting every time she was used. Why, she was almost like a prized hunting dog; only made of metal.

Christopher Taylor and his father had been treasure hunting together since the ten year old asked for a metal detector two Christmas's ago. Although his Christmas request was a total surprise to his father and mother, Paul had become fond of spending the spring and fall weekends with his son digging up treasure, that is to say, treasure according to Christopher. Most of the time it was just random pieces of old broken plows, nails or other objects that neither could identify; however, to Christopher these were his treasures that he had discovered all by himself. But today, it looked as if they might have stumbled on something "BIG." This day they were treasure hunting in a field where an old house had been many years ago. Although the house had been gone for a very long time, many of the older people in the town still remembered it and there were many tall tales of buried treasures on the grounds. So after securing permission to hunt on the property, Christopher and his dad were on their way.

"Keep digging son, can you see anything yet?" Paul asked excitedly.

No, not yet, I don't think I'm deep enough." Christopher replied.

Christopher kept digging trying not to look too excited to his father while trying to unearth the treasure. He was trying to remember to dig around the object just taking a plug of dirt out then exploring the dirt for whatever was in it. Although he had done this dozens of times, it was still hard not to just dig frantically until you hit something solid. One had to rely on his patience to do it right; a difficult thing to do for a ten year old. "Dad, I think I felt something."

"Good, can you see it yet; can you see what it is? "Paul quizzed.

"No, not yet but I'm getting close."

By this time both Christopher and his father were down on their knees digging frantically and sifting through the loose dirt from the round plug.

"It's got to be in here." said Christopher.

Just as he turned over the last piece of dirt a big bright silver object fell back in the hole against the dark freshly disturbed dirt. Christopher and his dad froze; each thinking the other was going to grab the treasure first.

"Go ahead son, you found it." Paul exclaimed.

With that said, Christopher reached down into the hole and pulled up a solid silver dollar. It was the largest coin he had ever seen, much less ever found.

"Wow, Dad, look it's a silver coin. This is the best thing I have ever found."

"Yeah son, let's look at the date and see how old it is." Paul answered.

The two hunters took the coin over to the truck where they had their water and a few snacks, just in case of the treasure hunters hunger attacks. Christopher's dad carefully washed the excess dirt off the coin to reveal a date of 1870. He couldn't believe how good the condition of the silver dollar was. It looked as though it had just been minted. By now, he was just as excited as Christopher.

"Well son, it looks like you have found a real treasure, lets go back to the house and look up the history on this coin, it's time for lunch anyway." Paul said.

"Yeah, and I can show mom and my friends. Dad, can I hold it on the way home?" Christopher inquired.

"Sure thing son, it's your treasure, the proud father answered.

Paul was smiling ear-to-ear knowing now Christopher was genuinely a hooked treasure hunter, just like himself. The two hopped into the truck and headed back home.

The Town

*P*aul's hometown of Summerville was nestled in a valley in the rolling foothills of a small mountain range off the beaten path far away from any big city. Summerville was a timeless town that was occasionally touched by the outside world. It was founded in the early pioneer days when a group of Settlers headed west, decided the valley was so beautiful, they would just stay and start a community. This is where Paul Taylor, his wife and three children lived. Although he did not realize it in his youth, Paul's boyhood was just about the kind you would read about in the story of Tom Sawyer. There was a crystal clear swimming hole full of fish, plenty of mountains to climb, neat places to camp out, and Paul had plenty of buddies to share his adventures with every summer; the kind of town where friends that were made in the first grade, were friends for life no matter what.

Summerville had been around over two hundred years and as it is in most small towns, the town's folk knew everyone else's business, but no one seemed to mind, mostly they just looked out for one another. Even the Mailman; Mr. Havercamp, was a local that everyone could set their clocks by. The big event every Saturday was going to the town square area and sharing news with your neighbors as you loaded up with groceries and supplies for the week. The old timers would sit and visit on the old benches in front of the stores and solve the world's problems in just a couple of hours. Every winter it snowed and produced a breath taking white Christmas. In fact, the town folks would joke with one another and comment on how no Christmas card had ever been produced that was as beautiful as their town. When the snow got too deep for the modern vehicles, many of the citizens would hitch up old horse drawn sleighs to get around and help their neighbors who couldn't get out. The summer evenings always had a cool breeze to top off the day, folks would still find time in the evenings to sit and visit on the porch or the tailgate of the old pick-up truck. There was the typical town square with the courthouse located in the middle, a drug store complete with soda fountain, community church on the outskirts of town, and of course the "FAIR" movie theater, where the town folks would see many classic movies long before they were classified as such. Mr. Fair would always save a few weeks in December to run everyones favorite "White Christmas" and "It's A Wonderful Life."

One, if not the favorite business on the square was the Farmer's Hardware Store run by a beloved veteran Allen Sanders and his son John. A friendly place with the reputation of having just about anything you could need for any project. All of the businesses still kept the Sabbath holy and closed on Sundays. Paul would go to sleep, as well as wake up, to the whistle of the No. 2 train that would bring in supplies and passengers to the town twice every day. Summerville was a great place to live. Paul's family had lived in Summerville for generations and he was the first of the Taylor's to leave home to go to college in another state. Sending his son off to college was the hardest thing he had ever done, but Paul's father could see the world was changing quickly and he wanted his son to be prepared with a good education. Leaving Summerville was not easy for Paul, but somehow he knew this was the right path for him to take. After he left, Paul realized how much he had taken the little town and its people for granted as he had done a lot of growing up during his time away from home. He realized even though Summerville was not a perfect place it was still a very unique place, blessed with people who even though their names and backgrounds were different would always watch out for one another.

Angela

After finishing college, Paul settled in the big city landing a great job with a sporting goods company, a position right up his alley, as he loved most any kind of sports. The position required much travel but that was one of the great things he liked about it. In fact, it was Paul's new job that introduced him to the sport of metal detecting. Paul met all kinds of people and traveled to interesting places, and on some occasions he would take some time out to test many of the company's metal detectors in a field or in the yard of an old abandoned house, after getting permission from the owner of the property of course. He settled in a small apartment and was well on his way to a successful career and was always quick to tell everyone he had the perfect job. One day on one of his sales trips, he met Angela. Angela was the purchaser at one of the stores that Paul called on regularly in his territory. Over time the two became very good friends and soon Paul could not wait to call on the store where she worked. In fact, he found himself having to visit a little more often after conveniently forgetting something and having to return. When it became obvious the two were in love, after about a year of courtship, they were married. Angela loved to hear about where Paul had grown up and could not wait to visit Summerville and meet his family and friends. Soon after they were married they did visit Summerville and to no one's surprise Angela did fall in love with the little town. The couple would visit on holidays and spend some of their vacation time there. Angela had always loved old houses, and Summerville was full of historical floor plans of every type. The one thing they all had in common is that they were all old and stately and still reflected a certain charm of the families that built them so many years before. It had been her dream to one day live in a beautiful Victorian style house with her family, and start a small business of her own or work as a teacher or librarian.

Moving Back Home

About two years after they had married, Paul and Angela found out the great news that she was going to have a baby. Just about the same time, Paul received a promotion at his company. The company was expanding and offered Paul a manager position with more territory. It just so happened the new territory included Paul's hometown of Summerville. To Paul and Angela this was an answered prayer. They had always planned on trying to find a house to live in rather than an apartment when they started a family. Paul wanted his children to experience the same small town upbringing and adventures he had growing up.

Upon hearing the news, Paul's family and the towns-folk began looking for a place for the couple to settle into. Housing was not plentiful in Summerville, but it just so happened upon hearing the news, Paul's Aunt Evelyn stepped up with an idea. She owned an old Pre Victorian home she had been renting out for years. She lived there during her early childhood. The old mansion was the old Summerville homestead built over one hundred and fifty years ago by the Summerville family, the first settlers in the valley and the founders of the town. As the years passed the house had been owned by many families but had fallen on hard times. In order to save the house from being torn down, Aunt Evelyn purchased it; however, it had become hard work and time consuming just to keep up with the maintenance with people renting the old place. The latest tenants had moved and she was looking to sell it to a nice family that could take care of it. Paul was very familiar with the place since he had spent many an afternoon playing with his cousins there; but he never dreamed he would ever have a chance to own the old place. He couldn't

wait for Angela to see it. He knew how much she had

always wanted a home they could call their own; espe-

cially an old historical mansion.

Aunt Evelyn

The townsfolk could hardly wait for Paul and Angela to move back. Most of them had watched Paul grow up, and all of them could tell a funny story on something that had occurred in his childhood. Other than Paul's parents, probably the most anxious was Paul's Aunt Evelyn. She, and her daughter, Joyce, owned Anderson's General Store in town. The store was almost as original as the day it was built. Paul's Uncle Forrest gave him his first job helping out in the summer and on Saturdays. Paul worked there from age twelve until he graduated from high school. During those years he learned many things about business and life, as the General store was the lifeblood of the community. Paul worked with his Uncle and his cousin Steve, whom he became very close to during those years. After he left Summerville for college, both his Uncle and cousin Steve passed away. Aunt Evelyn and her daughter Joyce, took over the responsibility of storekeepers.

During his visits to Summerville, Paul introduced his metal detecting hobby to Aunt Evelyn. Whenever he would come home, the two would always go out and see what kind of history they could dig up. Aunt Evelyn was fascinated by the machine but had no interest in operating it, she was just thrilled to see what, as she would put it "was under there." She would come up with some great places to hunt as she was born and raised in Summerville and knew the location of every old house and even where old log cabins had once stood, and she more than likely had a bit of history for every one of them. She could tell you what families, how long they had lived there and the name of their kids and probably their dog and cat's name. Her knowledge and memory never ceased to amaze everyone; especially Paul. One day the pair even dug up an old class ring one of her friends had lost fifty years before. It seems the lady was one of Aunt Evelyn's schoolmates and had been sick which caused her to loose enough weight that her ring fell off of her finger in her back yard. Neither one was ever able to locate it for years after even after thoroughly searching the area many times. Aunt Evelyn took Paul to the very place where the incident happened. After about thirty minutes of searching Old Betsy let out that unmistakable tone and the rest is history. Paul's satisfactions of that find that memorable day was only matched when Aunt Evelyn was able to present her old school mate her long lost class ring back to her over fifty years later. The incident even had a write up in the Summerville Falcon, the local newspaper which just happened to be the oldest newspaper in Tennessee.

Whenever they would get to treasure hunt, Paul enjoyed hearing about the history of the town and people, just about as much as the actual metal detecting, and Aunt Evelyn was a living history book.

The Surprise

Upon hearing Paul and his new wife were returning, Aunt Evelyn and Paul's parents got some of the towns people together for what she called a "Welcome back fix it-up party" repairing, painting, and doing whatever was needed to get the old place livable again. And, fix it up they did, when Paul saw it, he couldn't believe his eyes. He had never seen it look so good. Aunt Evelyn and the townsfolk considered it a wedding gift to the couple, with one stipulation; that they fill up the house with children, with them all having unlimited visiting privileges; of course. Paul had not told Angela that he had purchased the old house and he had a hard time keeping it a secret. But somehow, he pulled it off without a hitch. He had told her they would rent a small house outside of town until something came available and he would take care of everything not to worry, things would work out.

A few weeks after the house was ready, Paul and Angela drove to Summerville ready to settle in for good. On the way to what she thought was the temporary home. Paul made up a story that he had to stop and see Aunt Evelyn, to take care of some business.

As the couple pulled into the drive of the old mansion, Angela said, "Wow, your Aunt has sure fixed this place up. I have never seen it look so beautiful. Wouldn't it be great if someday we could have a house like this?"

Paul could hardly keep a straight face. "Yes honey, maybe someday we will," he replied, trying his best not to let her see the excitement on his face. Hey, let's go see if Aunt Evelyn is here yet."

The old Summerville mansion was built on one of the highest hills in town. There was a breathtaking view from all of the windows of the house, one side looking toward town and the other keeping watch over the valley. There was a porch practically surrounding the whole home. One could tell this use to be a central meeting place for many a get-together for any occasion. Paul parked on the side of the house trying to conceal the fact that there were a few more cars parked under the big hundred year old oak trees on the west side.

"Who do you think those cars belong to?" asked Angela.

"I don't know maybe Aunt Evelyn is still having work done on the house." Paul answered nonchalantly.

The two made their way up the front porch steps and on to the large front double door. Just as Paul was getting ready to knock, Aunt Evelyn opened the door.

"Come on in here, I thought you two had gotten lost." The three hugged and exchanged a little news in the front hallway. "Well come on in and make yourselves at home, and I really mean that." Aunt Evelyn was grinning ear to ear and even Paul was wondering what she had planned for the two. It was like she wanted to say something so bad and was so exciting she would burst, that's also the way Paul felt. He could hardly wait to tell Angela the big surprise that they would be living here soon.

The three walked a few steps into the huge mansion. The hallway was as wide as Paul remembered it from his boyhood, but even after a few steps inside he could not believe how the great the old place looked now just like stepping back in time. On the right side of the hallway the first room was a parlor which connected to a huge library with the most beautiful walnut book shelves, built from trees from a local forest, reaching from floor to ceiling, all full of old books.

"Now before you two start wandering around, I want to show you something." said Aunt Evelyn. She led them into the large living room on the left side of the hallway when just as they entered the room they were met with a Big "SURPRISE."

The huge room was chocked full of friends and relatives from all over the town. Angela could not believe it. Even Paul was impressed with everyone that had shown up. He could not believe what Aunt Evelyn had pulled off or even how she managed it without anyone spilling the beans.

After the shock had worn off a little, Angela was introduced to the folks she had not met, still carrying the look of total surprise through the whole ordeal while trying to remember names. Everyone was welcoming her to the town and offering any help she needed when the baby came. They all had brought food for a potluck lunch and as they all filled their plate and settled in visiting, it became a very nice afternoon and a great day for everyone.

After a few hours, the guest started saying their good-byes to head home. Aunt Evelyn whispered to Angela, "When everyone is gone, I'll give you the grand tour."

"That would be great. I've always wondered if this place was as beautiful on the inside as I imagined from Paul's description of how he and his cousin Walton would play here when they were boys." Angela replied.

After a few hours had passed and the couple had bid everyone goodbye for the day, Aunt Evelyn said, "Well Paul, should we tell her now or wait until we show her the whole place?"

"I think we should tell her now." Paul relied.

With that said, Paul turned to Angela with a question.

"Honey would you follow me outside to the porch?"

Looking bewildered but curious as to what he was up to, Angela agreed. The two made their way through the huge front double door. Paul said, "Now bear with me." And with that he picked her up and carried a giggling Angela back through the door and put her down on the other side of the door opening.

Angela asked, "What was that all about?"

"Welcome to our new home." Paul said with the biggest grin on his face she had ever seen.

"Our new home, what, what do you mean, I don't understand?" Angela questioned.

"Aunt Evelyn sold it to us." Paul said.

"You mean, it's ours to live in?" Angela questioned.

Paul and Aunt Evelyn both laughed. "I think that's what you do in a house."

"Oh Paul, I don't believe this, this is a dream, this is too much, I can't, I can't believe." With that Angela's eyes started to fill with tears of joy. She hugged Paul with the longest and tightest hug she had ever given him, then turned and hugged Aunt Evelyn.

"I think she kinda likes the place and she hasn't even seen the whole thing yet," said Aunt Evelyn as she patted Angela on the back.

With that, Angela asked, "Can I see the kitchen?"

Paul started laughing, "Typical woman."

"No honey, it's not what you think, please I have to see if something I've always dreamed about is there."

Well, sure Aunt Evelyn said, "Just follow me, I'll show you the fastest way to get there, this sound's important to me." Aunt Evelyn replied laughing as they walked.

The three rushed to the backside of the old house. Right before they reached the kitchen Angela stopped cold at the entrance.

"What's wrong?" asked Paul.

With tears streaming down her face, Angela pointed to the large arbor entranceway connecting the living room and kitchen. It was a half-moon arch about nine feet high and over three feet wide.

"This is what I have dreamed of, this is where I am going to mark on the wall how tall our babies get and there is plenty of room for three to be side by side." Angela cried. "Paul, this is the best present I will ever get in my life, a dream come true, thank you honey, thank you Aunt Evelyn, I love it and I love both of you."

Angela gave the both of them another big hug. Aunt Evelyn looked at Paul who had a big grin on his face.

"I would have never thought in a million years out of everything this old place has to offer that the archway would have been the one thing that attracted Angela most." Aunt Evelyn said laughing.

"That's true; I would have guessed it would have been the kitchen or the porch." Paul said.

They both looked at Angela with a tongue in cheek glance that triggered a laugh from all three as Angela wiped away her tears of joy again.

The Tour

"Well come on you two, I've been dying to show you what all the town folks have been keeping a secret from you all these months; let's go see the rest of the house." Aunt Evelyn said.

Her face beamed with delight as she led the two from room to room joyfully recalling memories of her own childhood spent in the old house. Of course, Angela had to stop again and look at the archway leading into the kitchen. The old home was a rare work of art by any standard, with wood working that was unmatchable The first floor had four huge rooms with the highest ceilings Paul and Angela had ever seen. The home was designed with a fireplace in every room including all four bedrooms upstairs. Each room was accessible from the hallway both upstairs and down. The double-wide staircase spiraled to the second level and as the three passed by, Angela commented how she could imagine someday her little girls coming down it on their wedding day. While touring the library, an object caught Paul's eye that was mounted over the fireplace. As he drew closer he realized it was Aunt Evelyn's favorite Uncles side-by-side shotgun that had been in the family for years.

"Aunt Evelyn, is that what I think it is; is that Uncle Babe's gun?"

"Why, yes it is. "Aunt Evelyn answered with a big grin. "I have always wanted you to have it since I can remember and you might as well enjoy it now, besides, it goes with the house perfectly. That's the very place Uncle Babe always kept it after hunting and I want you to take care of it now. Many a day that old gun was responsible for the food we had on the table." She recalled.

Paul was stunned and speechless. "I don't know what to say, I have always been fascinated with our family history and this is so much a part of it, thank you so much, I promise I will take good care of it." Paul replied.

"Oh I know you will, I'm just so happy you two are settling back in this town and especially in the old home place." Aunt Evelyn replied. "This place has so many memories for me and I know you will make some warm family memories yourself, and I am sure if Uncle Babe had lived to know you, he would agree. He was truly a man before his time so to speak. You know he started the General store that Joyce runs now, and she was going through some old papers and found some bills that customers were unable to pay during some hard times years ago, and he had written across them in big letters, "Jesus paid it all" and logged them as PAID IN FULL. He was a kind Christian fellow that helped people that had fallen on hard times, and when I say, a man before his time, why I remember as a young girl he tried to put together a vegetable train."

Paul and Angela looked puzzled, "What is a vegetable train?" They asked.

"Well, Aunt Evelyn answered, he had an old iron wheeled tractor and he hitched cotton trailers to it and filled them up with the vegetables the townsfolk had grown. He was planning to take the goods to the city in one big haul. You see, our country was in a depression, times were hard and he was trying anything to help the people of Summerville that did not have the transportation to take their fruits and vegetables to the market, it would have worked, but the state stopped him because his iron tractor tires tore up the roads so bad. That's just one of the many true stories about your Uncle Babe."

Aunt Evelyn quickly changed the subject. "But, come on now, I want to show you two the upstairs, it was always my favorite part of the house."

They reached the top of the stairs to arrive at another giant hallway with the four huge bedrooms across from each other. In between the bedroom doors an old antique table with a tall full-length mirror attached in the middle with an old felt covered chair on both sides of it. Aunt Evelyn paused for a moment in front of the mirror.

"You see that piece of furniture; whenever I see it, it makes me wonder how many beautiful young ladies stopped here to make a final check on their dresses and hair just before walking down those stairs to attend a party or greet some newly arrived guest or maybe meeting their future husband. Angela maybe in a few years you will be checking your daughter's wedding dress in front of the old mirror again." Aunt Evelyn said.

"I think that would be just wonderful." Angela replied.

That day, neither Paul or Angela could have ever dreamed, that in a few short years, they would be blessed, with not only a son, but two beautiful little girls. After exploring the first three bedrooms, Aunt Evelyn stopped at the last bedroom on the tour.

"You see that old heavy oak bed?" She asked. "When I was in my teens, my momma volunteered me to baby sit some of the children during the day while the parents worked; mostly in the fields. Well, I must have gotten a good reputation for babysitting, because, after a little time, I had a whole litter of kids here at once. I had so many babies I could hardly keep up with them all so I would put the end of their night gowns under that old poster beds leg, they had plenty of room to play and I didn't lose one kid my whole babysitting career. I don't think my Momma or Papa ever figured out how I managed all those kids and still got my own chores done." She said laughing. The three had a good laugh and proceeded down the end of the hallway. On the front side of the house was a door in the middle of the hall. After touring the bed-rooms Aunt Evelyn led them to the door and said, "Now I want to show you my favorite room in this old place." Aunt Evelyn took an old key from her pocket and unlocked the door. The trio made their way to the top of the stairs that revealed an octagon shaped room; it was almost like an attic within an attic. As Aunt Evelyn opened the door, the three were hit with the familiar pungent musty smell of a long forgotten cedar room. Each wall was fitted with the most beautiful stained glass windows that could be opened and secured on the inside of the wall. Although this was not the attic of the house, it still possessed a few old trunks and suitcases and an old dollhouse that was the exact replica of the mansion. On the back of the doll house an inscription read; "MADE IN 1870 BY CAPTAIN ZEBEDIAH SUMMERVILLE."

Paul and Angela were completely mesmerized with the whole atmosphere of the old place and noticed Aunt Evelyn even got quiet just taking in the old room probably revisiting her childhood memories of the place.

"This is the most beautiful and peaceful place in this house. "Aunt Evelyn remarked. "Yes, the memories I have playing here as a little girl, and listening to the grownups talk about the past. My mother and aunts and as many ladies as would fit would meet here, open up the windows and have quilting parties every Wednesday after their Bible Study. Why this is where I learned how to do everything from quilting to memorizing cooking recipes. I tell you what Angela, when you two get good and settled in, I would love to come over here and go through these old trunks and tell you about the history of this town and the people who use to trade stories here, if you like that sort of thing." Aunt Evelyn said.

"I would love it," said Angela.

Aunt Evelyn then turned to Paul and said. "Paul, you are welcome to join us."

Paul was still quietly studying every aspect of the room; then remarked. "You know how you live in a place all of your life and never notice things?" Both Aunt Evelyn and Angela nodded in agreement. "Well this is one of those things I never realized was here. All of those times as a little boy I played here, visited here, this house always reminded me of a castle from the outside, but I never knew that this was a room, I always thought it was just the attic." Paul said.

"This room hasn't changed much over the years because it has been locked and I have the only key." Aunt Evelyn replied. Her face was gleaming as she took

Angela's hand and gently placed the old key in her palm. "Now I'm passing it over to you to look after."

Aunt Evelyn then turned to Paul and said, "If you think this room is a curious place, come over here, I have something to show you that you will really like."

Then she directed Paul over to the other side of the room by a small table nestled against the wall. It looked like it was made for just that spot in the room and nowhere else, and as it turned out, it was. The custom built table was about three feet high and fit just under a piece of wainscot trim that divided the wall completely encircling the room. No one but Aunt Evelyn knew it was put there to hide something.

"Paul, help me move this table out a few feet." His Aunt instructed.

Paul grabbed one end of the table with Aunt Evelyn on the other and the two gently moved it out to the center of the room. Both Paul and Angela glanced at each other wondering what Aunt Evelyn was up to.

"Notice anything different about that section of the wall?" Aunt Evelyn quizzed.

Almost in harmony, Paul and Angela answered, "No, not really."

"Well, watch this."

With those words Aunt Evelyn put her hand under a section of the wainscot trim and pushed a hidden brass latch. With a little push and a pull, a whole section of the wall opened revealing a secret room.

The Secret Room

*A*s the door to the secret room opened it made a slight creaking sound, Paul and Angela stood frozen in speechless amazement.

"What is this?" they both exclaimed in harmony.

Angela and Paul slowly walked into the hidden space. There was no electric light but the angle of the sunlight from one of the windows beamed into the room illuminated the musty old space perfectly. The walls were made of cedar wood and totally bare except for the shelves reaching to the ceiling located on the back wall. The shelves had many old books and magazines, a stack of old newspapers and a couple of old antique cigar boxes that just at a glance, one could tell these items were of another time of long ago. There was also a little round table and an old oil lamp still half full of oil. Positioned next to the lamp was an antique typewriter that still had a sheet of now yellowed paper in it as if someone was planning to type something but was never started.

"This is a secret storage room." beamed Aunt Evelyn. "This house was built long before there were any Banks in Summerville. The original owners probably needed a place to hide money or valuables at one time or another, so they used rooms like this or the cellar for storage and other things. Summerville was not always as peaceful as it is today; there is a lot of history, good and bad that took place in our town. Uncle Babe showed me this room when we purchased the house from him and the folks he bought it from passed it to him. It is no telling how many of these old homes have these rooms and the people living there don't even know it. And come to think of it, I'm the only one living that knows about this one; that is until now." Aunt Evelyn said.

Paul was too busy studying the room in total amazement. He reached for a book that was slightly larger than the rest and pulled if off the shelf, the title read THE HISTORY OF SUMMERVILLE. He laid the old book on the little round table being very careful to not tear any of the pages he turned.

"This is unbelievable, this book has is the history of this town and county with names, dates and historical events of Summerville. I have been in our Library a million times and have never seen this book there." he exclaimed."

Aunt Evelyn interrupted. "That's probably because you're looking at the only one that exists, this one was written by the original owner of this house, Captain Zebediah Summerville; the founder of this town. I'll bet there is more history in this little room than in the whole town library."

"Well, I know where I am going to be spending my spare time for a while." Paul said, still scanning the old discolored pages.

And so he did. In the passing years, Paul and Aunt Evelyn would meet in the old tower and go through the pictures, documents and all the other items stored in the room. Many of the pictures took Aunt Evelyn back to her childhood and stirred memories she thought she had long forgotten, memories and stories Paul loved to hear about. Angela could not tell who enjoyed it more between the two. In the years to follow, these meetings became one of Paul's most cherished memories of his Aunt. The three came to an agreement that very day that they would keep the secret room and the treasures it had protected, just between them, at least until Paul and Angela's future family was old enough to appreciate how important all of these artifacts were, not only to their family, but everyone in the town.

Father and Son

On their way back to town from their successful treasure hunt, Paul and Christopher were still exciting about the silver coin find. To Paul, getting to spend time with his son just talking and answering questions about life was really his biggest treasure.

"Dad, who do you think the silver dollar belonged to?" Christopher asked, still examining it for any missed clues.

"You know son, that is a great question and that is one of the first things that runs through my mind every time I unearth a personal object that has been buried for so many years. I can tell by you asking that question you are going to be a great successful treasure hunter." Christopher paused for a moment.

"What do you mean dad?"

"Well son, you will understand better when you get older, but when I started metal detecting, one of the first things I would ask myself was, I wonder who this belonged to, or how long has this been lost or buried? It actually became more fun to try to find out the history on the treasure and who lost it as much as the thrill of digging it up." Paul said.

Christopher paused, still slightly confused from his father's explanation.

"Yeah, I guess I understand, but it sure is fun to find things."

Paul laughed out loud. "Yeah, it sure is and I repeat, you are going to be great at this and have a lot of fun, can you imagine finding a box full of gold coins and being known as Christopher the great treasure hunter. Why you would be known worldwide and be famous everywhere you went, you'd get the best table in the fast food restaurants, the best seat in the house at the

movie theater, people would be at your beckoning call."
Paul joked with a big smile.

"Yeah, right Dad," Christopher replied, sensing his father was having a little fun with him.

About that time, their homebound truck came over a hill and revealed an old run down mansion, almost equally as large as Paul's and Angela's home. It was the old Bailey home place. The house had been passed down in the Bailey family since it was built over one hundred and eighty years ago. It was more on the outskirts of town and at one time was one of the largest working cattle and horse ranches in the state. As it passed down from generation to generation many things had changed and for a many years the house was totally empty and had been nicknamed by most of the youngsters in Summerville as "The Old Haunted Bailey Mansion." Just recently, the heir of the old place came back to live there, the reclusive and mysterious Benjamin Bailey. Benjamin Bailey was a tall, tough looking thin man with tanned weathered skin. The folks of Summerville had not seen him for years and did not know much about him. He came back to town after mysteriously leaving many years prior and moved back into his old birthplace without any announcement. Ben was virtually a recluse. Paul, as well as many other people of the town had wanted to befriend Ben but he was known to keep to himself and only spoke when it was necessary. He would usually answer any questions with a short one-word reply and hardly ever started any conversations himself. Most of the townsfolk respected his privacy although still a bit nosey on where he had been all of those years. The only time he was seen was when he came to town for supplies. He had been frequently purchasing building supplies from John Sanders, the owner of the Farmer's Hardware store, fueling speculations he was repairing the old Bailey mansion. All of the kids of the town were scared stiff of him as he was slightly unkempt in appearance always wearing dark clothes and an odd looking large hat that would cover up much of his face. It was assumed he did not like children or anyone else not invited as "NO TRESPASSING" signs were nailed on every fence post around his house. It also didn't help the youngster's vivid imaginations or concocted rumors with Bailey always carrying an ax around with him when he would be in his yard.

As Paul and Christopher came closer to the Bailey mansion, Christopher seemed to be mesmerized by the old place.

"You know Dad that is a spooky old house, every time we pass it I get a real funny feeling. All of the guys are afraid to go near there when we go swimming because of the man that lives there now." Christopher said.

Paul was listening to Christopher as he to was fascinated with the old place and the owner, especially since he had found a very interesting article recently in an old Summerville newspaper stored in the secret room.

Paul had spent years carefully reading and documenting, especially the ancient newspapers his ancestors had saved. He had discovered many interested things, but one of the most mysterious incidents was the great stagecoach robbery that had occurred over one hundred years ago and directly mentioned the Bailey house in the article.

Paul turned to Christopher with one eye still watching the road.

"Son, How would you like to hear a real life unsolved treasure mystery that happened right here in this town?"

Christopher loved to hear his father tell him about history, especially if it was going to mean doing some metal detecting to find hidden treasure.

"Is this like the treasure hunting stories you read to me before going to sleep?" Christopher asked.

"This is even better because it really happened right here in this town over a hundred years ago, and as the story goes the mystery of the stolen gold has never been solved because the gold has never been found." Paul explained.

Paul could see by the look on Christopher's face, he was hooked already and this story had to be told and told now.

"You mean there could be some gold still buried near here?" Christopher quizzed.

"That's right son." Paul was even more anxious to tell Christopher the story as his wide eyed son was to hear it. Paul slowed the truck down, as he did not want to get back to the house before he finished the story. "Now son, before I tell you this, you and I need to have an agreement, because nobody else knows about this except me, so let's have a treasure hunter pact that you and I will not tell anyone else this story unless we check with each other first. This will be just our secret."

Christopher had a puzzled look on his face. "You mean I can't tell anybody, even my best friends Monte or Sam?"

"Especially Monte and Sam, Paul exclaimed, and after you hear the story you'll understand why." With that said, Paul reached out his hand toChristopher sealing the agreement with a handshake.

"Is it a deal?" Paul asked.

With a big curious smile on his face while shaking his father's hand, Christopher replied. "It's a deal dad."

"Well son, a few months ago, I came across some old Summerville newspapers. Some of these papers go back to the founding of our town and the best thing about them to me is they are full of history about Summerville and the people that helped to start our town. Way over a hundred years ago, even before the train came through town, Summerville was on a stagecoach route. The stagecoach would come through town around twice a month bringing in visitors, news from other towns, and many times new settlers to the area. It was a hard way to travel compared to the comfortable way we travel today, but at that time, it was the fastest and people could get to remote places the train did not go.Most of the travelers would rest up for a while and continue to their destination. This story centers around one person who stayed. His name was Jason Eckerd, a drifter that even to this day not much is known about his origin, and I was not able to trace his history, until a few days ago.

There was a picture of him in the paper which was very rare to do back then, but, considering what he did the publisher of the newspaper must have thought it was very important that people knew about him." Paul said.

"What did he do, what did he do Dad?" Christopher anxiously inquired.

At this point, Paul could see Christopher was already hooked on the story.

"Ok, I'll get to that part soon but first you need to know a little more about Jason Eckerd, the mystery man, as well as some history that I have managed to piece together through some research."

The Stage Coach Robber

*P*aul continued the story on their way home.

"When Jason Eckerd rode into Summerville those many years ago, nobody ever suspected he was planning to rob the stagecoach line of the payroll coming to the Summerville Bank and Trust. At that time most of the money was in gold coins and was delivered once every three months. Nobody in the town ever noticed Eckerd was observing everything from the scheduled days and times of arrival but also the best locations outside of town where he would have the best success of robbing the stage. He quickly blended into the town by getting a job at the Feed store as a laborer helping the farmers and ranchers load up their wagons with supplies. He even lived in a back room at the feed store. He was well liked and trusted by the family who owned the place, but, back to the story. Eckerd waited and observed almost six months before he finally made his bold move to rob the stage. He decided the best place to strike would be about two miles out of town, and that is exactly what he did. Eckerd had managed to steal a pistol from the hardware store the day before, unnoticed. On the morning of September 30th, 1876 he held up the stagecoach. According to the passengers and drivers of the coach, Eckerd was very nervous but unusually polite. There were bags of gold coins in a steal strongbox that was locked and tied on top of the coach. Eckerd forced the driver to open the box and he then took only two bags of coins, stuffing one bag in each saddlebag pouch. He then forced the driver to unhitch the horses from the stage apparently wanting to buy him some escape time. This is when things began to go wrong. The witnesses said the horses would not run off as planned so Eckerd fired his pistol in the air to spook them. Well, it worked but it also spooked Eckerd's horse, which ran off before Eckerd could secure the gold on the saddle; leaving him to escape on foot with two heavy bags of gold coins. As he ran up a hill on foot the driver retrieved his shotgun and fired at Eckerd slightly wounding him in the foot but not enough to stop him from escaping with the loot."

"Sounds like a TV show Dad," exclaimed Christopher, still hanging on every word of the story.

Paul laughed. "Yes it does son, in fact I think they get some of their stories from old records like this; but just wait, I haven't gotten to the best part yet."

As their pickup truck entered the long winding drive leading to home, Paul hurried to finish the story before entering the house.

"What happened next Dad?" exclaimed Christopher anxiously.

"Well, the stage driver managed to get back to town after rounding up the team of horses, then, the sheriff and some townspeople with the stagecoach driver guiding them, went back after Eckerd. By this time it was mid- afternoon, the sheriff managed to track Eckerd to a farm near here and captured him in a barn."

Paul looked over at Christopher. "Can you take a wild guess at whose barn it was, son? "Christopher took a deep breath while in deep thought, and then his face lit up. "Dad, was it the old Bailey barn?"

Paul laughed out loud, "You're a pretty good detective and listener; you're right, it was the old Bailey barn and you know as well as I, it is still standing today."

"But Dad, what about the gold?" Christopher anxiously asked. Paul turned off the truck leaned back in the seat and paused taking a deep breath. "This is where the story really gets mysterious and I am having trouble finding any details. According to the articles written in the following newspapers, the gold was never found and Eckerd refused to reveal where he had hidden it. Do you remember I told you I could not find anything about Jason Eckerd in the historical documents?"

Christopher gave a positive nod and replied, "Yes, I do at the beginning of the story."

"Well it turns out the sheriff found out that Jason Eckerd was a phony name, his real name was none other than Samuel Bailey, a distant relative of Ben Bailey here in Summerville. This opened up a whole bigger can of worms with a bunch of unanswered questions. From here, I had to fill in some of the blanks myself and speculate what happened after Bailey was captured and try to piece things together the best I could."

Paul paused for a few seconds then turning to Christopher. "Hey, maybe you can help me find some answers in this mystery."

"Wow Dad, that would be great, but how can I find out anything?" Christopher inquired.

"Well, I'm going to help you, we will do it together, I can tell you want to help me solve this mystery of the hidden gold and I think we can have some fun while doing it. I have a whole stack of old newspapers that I know are full of undiscovered clues just waiting to be discovered." Paul exclaimed.

"When can we start searching Dad?" An excited Christopher questioned.

"Very soon, but there is something even more important we have to do first." exclaimed Paul.

"What's that Dad?" Christopher asked anxiously.

Paul raised his head up and took a deep breath.

"You smell that son?" he asked half smiling."

"Sure do Dad. "Christopher quipped.

"That's the glorious aroma of your mother's bacon and coffee and I see she is coming out on the porch now to call us in for what I think will be a delicious treasure hunters breakfast.

"Oh yeah, I almost forgot, I can't wait to show her the silver dollar we found." Christopher replied. His faced beamed as he once again pulled out his treasure to examine it and show it to his mother. He had managed to rub all of the dirt off of the old coin; now it almost looked like new. As the two walked up the porch steps, Paul put his arm around his son's shoulder.

"You handled that metal detector like a real pro today, your mother is going to be proud of you, just like I am son." exclaimed Paul.

Even though Paul loved to find treasure when he and Christopher would hunt, his private talks with his only son was what he truly enjoyed more than any treasure he could ever dig up. It had been a very good day.

Questions

*I*t was early spring in Summerville and Paul had been making many trips to the secret room. He was slowly taking on the task of documenting all of the historical papers and postcards the ancestors of the house had stored over the years. He was so glad that all of these items had been saved. It was going to take him many years to actually read and classify all of the items. Since discovering the article in the Summerville Falcon's paper on the stagecoach robbery he had been concentrating on finding all of the old newspaper articles putting them in order. There were so many of them stacked in one of the corners of the secret room, they almost reached to the top of the ceiling. It didn't matter to Paul, this was something he enjoyed; it was history.

There were so many unanswered questions concerning

the gold heist that were running through Paul's head.

Why had Samuel Bailey changed his name? Why had

no one recognized him as a Bailey in the town until after

the robbery? Then there was the most mysterious ques-

tion of all. Had anyone ever found the gold and kept it

secret, or was it still hidden somewhere on the Bailey

place? This was Paul's personal mission, to find the

answers to these questions and many others that were

sure to come up. He was looking forward to working with

his new partner. One of his prayers was Christopher

would learn to love history as much as he did.

Memorial Hill

When spring came to Summerville it was an exciting and busy time for everyone. For the farmers, it was planting the new crops, for the ranchers it meant keeping tabs on newborn calves and colts, for Paul, it was his favorite time of the year just being able to enjoy the weather while taking notice of everyone getting busier preparing for upcoming seasons. Everything seemed new and refreshed. Spring was announced by nature in multiple ways but probably the most beautiful manner was in the unbelievable flowers and plants that would start to "show off" as the locals would say, all over the town. One particular place was a hill not really tall enough to be called a mountain, offset maybe a half-mile from town but was visible from both entrances of Summerville for many miles. What made the hill special was it was entirely covered with mysterious and colorful flowers of all types. The very sight of the hill would take your breath away. Most species of the colorful plants were still a mystery to the town folks that were considered experts on plants. There were no duplicates anywhere in the state as far as anyone knew. It was speculated that many had been brought from overseas, as they were not native to America. Some had been planted over the years by surviving relatives that had lost a family member in the wars that had occurred since America's birth, but a majority of the plants were still a head scratcher of how they got there. The hill was respectfully known as Memorial Hill. For the spring, summer and much of the fall until the first hard freeze Memorial Hill would almost glow with the most beautiful colors ever witnessed by the naked eye. People just passing through town would sometimes stop the locals on the street and inquire about the hill. One day a professional photographer came through town asking permission to put a picture of Memorial Hill on the cover of a book of the most beautiful places in America. He told the townsfolk that in all of his years of traveling he had never seen such a beautiful and peaceful sight. All of the people of Summerville agreed with him. Still, to Paul Taylor, the hill was a mystery that he would someday love to solve.

Bobi Stone

efore Paul and Angela married and made the final move to Summerville, Angela worked for a large company in the city. Many days at lunchtime she would just walk and kill time at the local shops that were near. One place she loved to frequent was a small art and framing gallery located in a row of quaint shops and restaurants. A lady named Bobi Stone owned the business and most if not all of the paintings were her own work. Angela would lose all track of time just reviewing her work, as they were all beautiful and very unique. Even though Miss Stone dealt with the public every day Angela noticed she was not the friendliest person she had met, and she mostly kept to herself.

Angela attributed it to just being shy or slightly withdrawn when it came to dealing with people in general. Maybe it was just her business persona she wanted to project to the public. That all seemed to change after Angela started small conversations with Bobi and purchased one of her paintings of a beautiful landscape. Eventually the two became friends and Angela would later learn that Bobi Stone was an only child and her parents had met a tragic untimely death that left her with no other family. In one of their conversations, Angela happened to mention how she was going to move to the beautiful little town of Summerville and suggested Bobi might find some great landscapes to paint and invited her to visit her and Paul. Bobi seemed slightly interested but soon the conversation led to other subjects and was all but forgotten.

After Paul and Angela had been married about a year, a knock was heard on their door and Angela was surprised to see Bobi Stone on the other side. This was just the first of many visits when she would stay and paint a few of the town's unique landscapes and travel back home to the city. After a few visits Bobi fell in love with the town and decided to become one of the new citizens of Summerville. She had grown tired of the city and just wanted to spend her time painting and framing her work. Angela made her a place in her little antique shop and soon she had plenty of work as the people of Summerville began to recognize her talent not to mention the already established clientele she had all over the country.

After Bobi Stone had completely settled in, Angela noticed a nice change in her. She became one of the friendliest and happiest people any one would ever want to meet. It seems Bobi Stone had started a new life with her new adopted family; the good people of Summerville.

Monte and Sam

pring meant a lot of different things to the town folks, but for Christopher and his friends it meant school was out soon and summer vacation was near. Now Chris, as he liked to be called by his buddies had many friends, but his best friends were Monte Burns and Sam Coates. The three had been close since the day they learned how to talk and summertime meant many new adventures were ahead. Paul would often comment on how you hardly ever saw one without the other two not too far behind. Monte Burns and Sam Coates were as different as night and day. Monte was the most level headed one of the group. He liked to think things out and sometimes when he would get quiet, Christopher and Sam would know he was planning something. Sam on the other hand was the "devil may care" type, always speaking his mind before thinking and asking many questions just about anything and everything. Most of his Christmas toys usually ended up being taken apart just for him to see how they worked, however he always managed to get them back together in workable order somehow to his parent's amazement.

Monte's father raised vegetables for the market on his farm just outside of town and Sam's father raised cattle and horses. He owned three ponies that the boys learned to ride quite well. This particular summer Monte's father offered the boys a part time job helping bring in some of the crop. The boys were very excited about making their own money and they did very well learning the work ethic as their fathers would often say. And worked they did. After a hard morning of picking vegetables the three would hop on their bikes and go swimming in the creek, passing Benjamin Bailey's place each way. There wasn't a day that went by that Christopher did not think about looking for the possible hidden gold. Over the past two years he had gotten his buddies interested in treasure hunting also. It worked out good for him as he would find the items and Monte and Sam would dig them up. The more they hunted the more Monte and Sam became hooked on metal detecting, especially when they would find a coin or two. Christopher had explained to them what his dad's rules were for searching on private property and Monte and Sam seemed to have no problem with asking permission; that is except from Benjamin Bailey whom all three were deathly frightened of.

Every day they would pass by the Bailey mansion, Sam would relentlessly try to convince Christopher to carry out a plan to sneak into Ben's yard without asking. You see, all three boys were petrified of Benjamin Bailey and none of them had the courage to talk to him much less ask if they could treasure hunt on his land.

Benjamin Bailey's yard was unkempt and actually looked scary even to grownups. There was hardly a square inch on the house that the paint was not peeling off. There was a fence that went almost all around the house. Many of the boards were missing or about to fall off. The yard had loose brush and tall weeds growing in clumps. The rest of the yard consisted of loose sandy dirt. And if there was any doubt that Benjamin Bailey did not want visitors, all you had to do was read the NO TRESPASSING signs nailed to every corner of the dilapidated fence. And to make matters worse, there was that scary ax that Ben Bailey always carried around with him when out in his yard. Needless to say the three did not waste any time speeding up on their bikes to get by the old house as fast as they could trying to pretend not to see Benjamin Bailey as they passed.

The Tree House

One of the best places the boys liked to hang out was the huge tree house that Paul, Ted Burns and John Coates teamed up to build for their boys. Paul had secured tree house plans from his company and the three fathers made a Boy Scout project of building a one of a kind house. They included Christopher, Monte and Sam in the project as well as the rest of the boys in the pack, in which they were rewarded with a Boy Scout badge to put on their uniforms. The truth was, the fathers had more fun building it than any of their sons. They picked out the largest old oak tree on the place not too far from the house, which was thought to be one of the oldest and largest in town, and did a very good job building what became a must see for many of the ole timers in town. It was the largest tree house most people had ever seen designed complete with a singled roof and walls open at least four feet down from the roof with operational shutters that could open and close to accommodate a cool breeze. The view from the structure was breathtaking. It was complete with a rope latter, trap door and even a sign that read "NO GIRLS ALLOWED." Of course that did not stop Christopher's little sisters, Arielle and Alyssa from sneaking up from time to time. Many times in the late afternoon, Angela would find Paul, John and Ted in the tree house themselves acting like they were still in grade school talking about old times while admiring their building skills. Angela and the other wives would just smile and shake their heads realizing, you just can't take the boy out of the man. And if they truth were known they really did not want to.

Over the following years the tree house served the boys well as it was considered their official clubhouse.

Many summer adventures were planned and carried out there. Although not visited very often now, the tree house still stands to this very day.

The Final Clue

It was mid summer now and Paul was using most of his spare time in the evening carefully reading every word in the old Summerville Falcon newspapers looking for some clue to what could have happened to the stolen gold. He had to be very careful as not to damage them as some of the pages were starting to get brittle with age. Still, taking their age into account, Paul was amazed at how well they had survived. He had stressed to Christopher the importance of being very careful with them, especially when he would turn the pages. One evening as the two were searching, Christopher discovered a headline that caught his eye. It read, "STAGE COACH ROBBER DIES IN JAIL."

Christopher called to Paul in an excited voice.

"Dad, I think I found something, come here and look at this."Paul rolled his chair across the pine floor next to Christopher and began reading out loud the heading. Paul could feel his heart about to pound out of his chest. He began to read it out loud. "A one Samuel Bailey who was using the alias name Jason Eckert died in jail today of an infection caused by a shotgun wound he acquired as he tried to make a getaway. Bailey was caught on the Bailey ranch after he robbed the Summerville Stage Line two months ago. He was wounded in the leg in which an infection and fever set in soon after his capture." Paul was trying not to miss a single word of the article in his excitement but was reading very fast. Then, at the bottom of the article he found the words he had been searching for, for months. "BAILEY NEVER REVEALED THE LOCATION OF THE STOLEN GOLD AND AS OF THIS PRINTING THE GOLD HAS NOT

BEEN FOUND." Paul leaned back in his chair and put his arm around Christopher.

"Son, you did it, you found the article we have been looking for; the final clue. Do you realize what this could mean? That stolen gold could be still somewhere on the Bailey farm."

Christopher produced a quick smile then sunk in his chair and produced a concerned look that Paul immediately noticed.

"What's wrong son, this is great news don't you agree?"

Christopher let out a big sigh, "But Dad, it's on the BAILEY place." By now, Paul was coming back to his senses from the excitement of the article. He realized Christopher had a good point as he rested his face in both of his hands with his elbows propped on the table.

"Well son, it looks like we have another slight problem on our hands".

"Sure does Dad." Christopher replied.

Cousin Walton

everal days had passed since Christopher had discovered the article on the stolen gold. For Paul, it had answered many of his questions but there were still many more that needed investigation. The main question that kept haunting him was; had someone found the gold and just made off with it? Paul was convinced there were more answers in the old newspapers. He and Christopher continued to search as much as they could. Then Paul noticed there was about an eight-month gap in the published dates on the papers. He wondered if his ancestors had just failed to save them or was there another reason for this added mystery. Paul was going to have to go on a business trip soon for a week and he desperately needed to find some answers.

He decided to go see his closest cousin, Walton Griffin.

Walton Griffin had grown up with Paul. He too was a native of Summerville and lived there until his family moved to another state. However, that did not hinder Walton from coming and staying every summer with his Aunt Evelyn and Cousin Joyce. Aunt Evelyn held a very special place in her heart for her brothers child and the two spent many days together every summer. Walton became an expert on everything from family history to growing a garden. Ask him any question about past relatives and he could tell you a colorful story. It would amaze Paul when he would talk about the past family history. Paul was convinced Aunt Evelyn had the perfect person in Walton to carry on the family legacy.Paul could not wait until Walton would come back to visit each summer. The two became like brothers as they grew up together. For a few years they lost contact when Walton went to college, married and started his family. He earned a law degree and to everyone's delight moved back to in his hometown for good. When the Summerville newspaper went up for sale, Walton purchased it and ran a very respectable business. Walton was the perfect owner as he wanted the paper to keep the tradition it had been famous for over one hundred and fifty years and that suited everyone in the town just fine. Paul had decided to take Walton into his confidence on the stolen gold story and see if he had run across any historical documents that could help him. Now, since Walton loved history as much as Paul, he was totally captivated by the story. He immediately started research on the missing papers and came to find out the Summerville Falcon had caught on fire many years ago along with the Courthouse; both buildings were totally destroyed along with all historical records up to the year 1878. For almost a year the paper went out of print. Walton was not familiar with the stagecoach robbery and did some additional research for Paul to help speed things up a bit. What he found was even years later nothing had been printed about the missing gold. This meant Paul probably had the only documents in existence that told the story of the stage coach robbery. Walton agreed to keep the story mum out of respect for Paul's wishes and the two agreed that if the word got out of buried gold somewhere near it would be a nightmare for Ben Bailey dealing with trespassing treasure hunters on his land. He did ask Paul a favor that if he ever found the gold to let him have the exclusive scoop to do a write up on the story. Paul replied by also promising him all of the old papers he had with a tour of the secret room. The newspapers needed a safe home and Paul and Walton agreed that is where they belonged. The two had about an hour of good catching up conversation and laughs of old times then said they're good buys promising to get together when Paul returned from his business trip. Paul was feeling even better now about the missing gold still being buried somewhere near Summerville.

The New Detector

*P*aul's company would always assign him to test the new line of metal detectors before marketing them to the public. After he had fully tested them in the field he submitted his comments and review to a treasure hunting magazine to publish. Paul would include Christopher in the test as much as possible. He would get Christopher to use the detector and find an object then he would record the depth of the object, a description as in the size and what kind of soil it was in. It was an easy task as well as great fun for the two. It also helped Christopher to become an expert at the sport. The latest model Paul was testing was the new Gold Duster. It was supposed to be the latest and greatest with all of the gadgets anyone could imagine. Actually, it was a good product and Paul and Christopher liked how simple it was to use. The Gold Duster left no guess-work on what the treasure was. It still had very sensitive headphones to help identify whether it was a coin or iron or just basic junk by the tone. But this model was different. It had a screen built in on the end in which a needle would verify if you had found iron, copper, silver or even gold. It even described the type of coin you had discovered and how deep the item was buried. In Paul's review of the Gold Duster for the magazine, he said "this machine does everything but feed you lunch." The name came from the claims it was so sensitive to objects, that it could even detect the smallest amount of gold dust. Needless to say, it was a very impres-sive machine and it did the job very well and ultimately became a very good seller.

The Business Trip

The time had finally arrived for Paul to leave on his business trip to the home office. Paul use to love to travel, however, as his family became older as well as himself, he found himself losing the desire to be away from them and his friends even if it was for only a week or so. He would hop the train on Sunday and be back home the next Friday if all went well.

Leaving his family was more difficult to do each time he had to go. Paul would tell Christopher, Arielle and Alyssa to take care of their mom and stress to his son he was the man of the house until he returned; with special instructions to take care of his mother and sisters. This always made Christopher feel grown up and he took his instructions very serious. As Paul was leaving he reminded Christopher to remember the "treasure hunters creed" if he wanted to use the new metal detector.

"I remember Dad; always ask the owner's permission and leave the ground better than it was before you started." He replied.

With a few more reminders and hugs and kisses to everyone, Paul was off to the big city for a week.

The Plan

The summer days were full for Christopher, especially since he had started his summer job in the vegetable and fruit garden. Everything was getting ripe and ready to pick so it kept Christopher and his buddies very busy. Still, they only had to work half a day for Monte's father and had the rest of the day free to play. Most every day they would go swimming, with Sam and Monte still pressuring Christopher trying to convince him to sneak into Ben Bailey's yard to treasure hunt every time they would pass Bailey's house. "Just think, Sam would say; there is probably all kinds of valuable treasure in scary old Bailey's yard, why do you think he is out there so much with an ax and has so many no trespassing signs out? Now is the best time to go since your Dad is out of town."

Sam and Monte would not let up and as the days went by, their argument started making more sense; finally Christopher agreed that they would all sneak into Ben's yard to see what they could find. Christopher knew deep down that this was wrong and just hoped nobody would ever find out; especially his father. A few days later, the three met in the tree house to hatch a master plan to sneak into Ben Bailey's yard the next afternoon. They agreed Christopher would operate the metal detector while Sam and Monte would quickly dig up any and everything that registered as valuable not wasting time on junk readings. Christopher would use the headphones on the detector in order to hide the sound of discovered objects. Only he would be able to hear the tones of discovered treasure. They would enter through the missing fence slats around the back part of the house and hopefully not be seen or heard by scary Benjamin Bailey. If they found anything, they would meet back at the tree house. Sam and Monte made it all sound so simple and easy but they were about to find out things don't always go as planned.

Run

The next day Christopher was feeling very uneasy about the whole plan Sam and Monte had hatched but he knew if he chickened out now he would probably never hear the end of it. Besides, he too was very curious as to what might be in Ben Bailey's yard, especially since they had discovered there could still be hidden gold near Ben's house. Even though he had come close to spilling the beans several times, Christopher had done a good job of keeping the secret of the hidden gold, especially from Sam and Monte.

The treasure hunters had decided to strike on Thursday afternoon and enter through the broken and rotting gate boards on the more hidden side of Ben

Bailey's yard. First they made their way hiding behind the mammoth oaks trees on the outskirts of the yard. When they had made their way outside of the fence, they noticed a large tree that was almost blocking the view from the house. The boys squeezed through the old fence and all took a position behind the tree. "You guys watch for me and try to stay hidden behind the tree, if I get a reading I will point to where you need to dig." Christopher exclaimed.

Sam and Monte agreed and stuck close together facing Christopher who had his back toward Ben Bailey's house. Christopher then plugged in the headphones to the base of the Gold Duster and set the machines volume making himself the only one that could hear the tones if something was detected. He also short-ened the telescopic wand that attached the base and circular detecting head on the end; making it easier to sweep. He slowly started to sweep the detector back and forth trying to keep it as close to the ground as possible. It was only a few minutes when he started to get a strange reading and tone. Christopher looked at the meter to see where the needle was pointing. It has settled between gold and silver but not on the coin reading. He passed over the buried object several more times each time clearing the reading to make sure it was not a piece of worthless junk. Each time the tone was deep and pure and the needle on the readout went to the same place. At each sweep Christopher would get more excited but still puzzled by the reading. After pinpointing the location of the object he signaled to his friends where to dig.

Christopher laid the Gold Duster to the side to help his buddies dig. "Be careful not to poke it with the digger." He instructed.

Sam hit something with his digging tool and motioned to Christopher to help. Christopher brushed away the sand like soil and uncovered a small box that was hardly even buried at all. He was so enthralled in his find he did not notice the look of total fear on the faces of his cohorts in crime. When he did look up, Sam and Monte were white as ghost and were quickly scooting in a backwards crawl trying to get their balance to get to their feet and run. Then, a stern voice yelled out "DON'T MOVE BOYS" at the same time Christopher felt a strong boney hand on his shoulder that pushed him off to his left knocking him off balance snatching the headphone plug out of the Gold Duster. The force of the headphone's coiled wire and plug in coming out of the detectors base was so hard it whipped around Christopher's body twice. While Christopher was attempting to regain his balance he managed to glance halfway over his shoulder just in time to see the silhouette of an ax in the air. He then heard and felt a thud right next to his side with the ax head sinking its sharp edge deep into the ground. Chunks of earth hit him on his sweaty face and neck making their way inside his shirt with bits of earth pelting him in his eyes. Petrified with fear and just desperate to escape he managed a rapid crawl then lifted himself on to his feet and finally tore through the open boards on the fence with the headphones still on his head and the treasure box held tightly in his left hand. He had never run so fast in his life. His speed was only matched by the raw fear circulating in his mind and his rapid heartbeat. The metal tip of the headphones was flying from side to side behind him skipping on the dirt and pebbles on the rural road. Christopher ran so fast he caught up with Sam and Monte and passed them with ease. None of the boys could utter a word they were so out of breath. Staying true to the second half of the plan they made a beeline for the tree house and safety.

After reaching the tree house the three leaned against the tree to rest with their hearts pounding out of their chest. Sam was the first to speak. "Did you see Ben Bailey, did you see he, he, tried to chop us up with his ax?"

Monte was still panting faster a thirsty hound dog chasing a rabbit.

"Where did he come from?" He demanded.

"I don't know, I just looked up and he was there."
Replied Sam.

Ignoring his friend's statements, Christopher answered angrily. "You guys were supposed to keep a look out for, for." Christopher then stopped talking in mid-sentence suddenly realizing his worst nightmare.

"OH NO, I left the metal detector, I left the metal detector in the yard." He shouted. "Ben Bailey has my Dad's new metal detector."

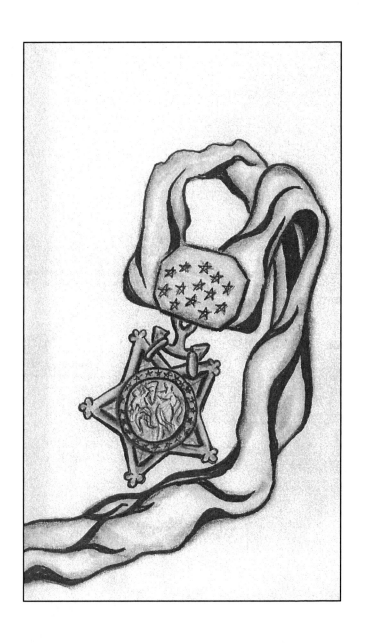

That Sick Feeling

The next morning, Christopher asked Angela if he could stay home from the vegetable field saying he felt sick. He had hardly gotten any sleep worrying about what had transpired in Ben Bailey's yard. Sam and Monte stopped by on their way to work but neither boy hardly mentioned the botched treasure hunt and did not even ask what was in the box that Christopher had now lost any curious notions to open. All three were noticeably silent and were thinking the same thing. What was going to happen when their parents found out?

That Friday afternoon, Paul returned from his business trip in a very good mood thankful to be back home with his family and looking forward to hearing how everyone's week had gone. The family would usually discuss things over a big meal at the end of the day, something Christopher always looked forward to until now. They were about half finished with supper when Paul told Christopher he had found a great place to go on their weekend treasure hunt. Paul noticed Christopher's reaction was less than enthusiastic. Christopher normally would interrogate Paul the rest of dinner time asking questions, so when his reaction was just a couple of words, Paul knew something was wrong. Christopher hardly ate anything and asked if he could be excused to go to his room after supper. After he left, Paul questioned Angela as to what was wrong."He said he was sick, but I think there is something else bothering him; I've never seen him act this way." Replied Angela.

"I think your right; I'm going to find out what is wrong, I've never seen him like this either." Paul replied.

Later, Paul went to Christopher's room to see what the matter was. As he entered the room, Paul found his son sitting on his bed with a sad and worried look splashed all over his face. He had never seen his son act like this and now he was becoming concerned.

"Son, are you feeling sick, is there something I can do for you?" Paul questioned.

Christopher could not stand it anymore. Tears welled up in his eyes and he began to tell Paul the whole story of the Ben Bailey botched treasure hunt. Paul sat on the bed and restrained himself from interrupting the confession. When Christopher was finished Paul paused a moment taking it all in, all the time trying to plan what he was going to say to his son. Paul took a couple of deep breaths.

"Well son, I have to say that I am really disappointed in you for disobeying my wishes and trespassing on Mr. Baileys's property. You know that you're going to have to be punished." Paul exclaimed.

"Yes Sir, I understand." Christopher answered. It was a very odd thing but Christopher felt better just confessing to his father and at that time was not concerned about being punished or even worried about what the punishment was to be. He was just relieved he had told his father the whole story."But what that punishment will be is what I am going to have to think about." said Paul in a stern voice that was mixed with disappointment.

That's when Christopher started to get concerned. He did not like this strained relationship with his father. It was his father's disappointment in him that was the worst feeling he had ever had.

"Dad, there is something else." Christopher hopped off of the bed and went to his dressers top drawer and pulled out the box he had uncovered from Ben's yard and handed it to Paul."What is this?" Paul inquired. "I don't know, I haven't opened it yet, I was feeling so bad about what I did, it just didn't matter to me what was in it." Christopher confessed.

Paul took the dirty felt covered box and slowly opened it. He could not believe what he saw. It was a medal. The most beautiful military medal Paul had ever seen. After a couple of seconds, Paul realized Christopher had dug up a Congressional Medal of Honor. Paul then asked himself, what was a Congressional Medal of Honor doing buried in Ben Bailey's back yard?

Fatherly Advice

Paul kept the medal with him. The next day he decided to go visit his father who lived just across town on the same ranch where he grew up. Paul would often stop by to check on his parents and sit and visit with his Father and Mother. This time it was different. Paul was still very upset with Christopher and needed some fatherly advice.

Paul's father was James Bennett Taylor, one of the most respected and loved men Summerville had ever produced. You could be assured if anyone needed help of any kind; JB was usually the first one there. He was a veteran of two wars but hardly ever discussed his battle scars or his time in the service of his country. The only thing he loved more than his hometown and country was God, his family, and his grandchildren. Christopher was his first grandchild and they were very close. From the minute Paul entered the house, James could tell there was something bothering his son. After a few minutes when they both were comfortable, James questioned Paul as to what was on his mind. Paul told his father the whole story of what had transpired with Ben Bailey, even the part about the ax and Christopher thinking Ben was trying to kill him. He showed his Dad the Congressional Medal of Honor Christopher had found. Surprisingly to Paul, his father did not seem surprised at the find.After Paul finished the story, James rose slowly out of his chair and walked over to the picture window that held a beautiful view of Memorial Hill. Still staring out the window without turning around seemingly deep in thought, Paul's father responded.

"You know son, every time I see Memorial Hill, I think about Ben and a host of many brave men. You probably don't know this but Ben and I grew up together as best friends. It's funny, when I see Christopher and his friends playing, paling around together and even getting into trouble like what you just described, it takes me back to mine and Ben's adventures. We even left to go to war together, left on the same day with thirteen other guys from our little town and other small towns in the county. One of these days I'll tell you some of the mischief we got into. I usually keep up with Ben but since he got back into town I haven't contacted him, with all of the extra work I've had lately, so I'm overdue to call him." JB paused for a moment; then began to speak again.

"Son, I can tell you this with certainty; Ben would not hurt a fly. He has had a lot of tragedy in his life over the last few years; some things he has talked about, others, he has chosen to keep to himself. One thing I know; Benjamin Bailey is a good man and has always been a true friend. Now, as far as my grandson is concerned, we both know he is a good boy with an honest heart; however, he does need to learn a lesson of life from this incident. I trust you enough to do the right and the fair thing with him, and my heart tells me by the look on your face you already know what you're going to do; and whatever that is; it is not going to be easy for you, or Christopher. Paul, you are a good father and a son that I am proud of. You have raised Christopher wisely by being an example for him to follow. I know things are going to work out in this, just have faith."

Paul stood up from his chair and started walking toward the door.

"You know Dad, your right, I think I have known how to handle this from the start, but it made it better to talk about it with you."

James put his arm around Paul's shoulder and walked with him to the door. "Tell you what Paul; I can give Ben a friendly call if you like."

Paul nodded his head in agreement. "I would appreciate that."

Paul paused for a moment. "Dad, would you do something else for me?" Paul humbly asked. Paul turned facing his father.

"What's that Son?" JB replied.

"Would you pray for me that I will do the right thing?" Paul asked.

James Taylor put his strong rough hands squarely on Paul's shoulders and looked him square in the eye.

"Son, I have been praying for you from the day you were born."

Paul could hardly hold back his tears as he had sensed something different about his father on this visit. He grabbed his father and they gave each other a big hug.

"Thanks Dad." Paul replied. As the two made their way out on the porch, James Taylor repeated his words to Paul.

"Remember Son, Ben is a good man."

It was only around a year later that James Bennett Taylor's spirit stepped into heaven to meet the Lord he had chosen to serve since he was eighteen years of age. The whole town of Summerville closed their doors to say goodbye at the little white church on the hill at the edge of town. The people of the town felt like they had lost a part of themselves. It was the saddest day Paul had ever known in his life. And sitting on the front row to say a final farewell to his longtime friend, was Benjamin Bailey.

The Decision

*P*aul felt much better after his talk with his father. He had decided that Christopher was going to have to go over to Ben's house and apologize for trespassing on his property, give him back his medal and retrieve the Gold Duster. Satisfied that Ben was not trying to hurt his son but also still curious what was going on with the ax, Paul planned to talk with Christopher when he got home. He knew this was going to be hard for him, but he needed to learn a lesson from this whole mess. Meanwhile, the fathers of Sam and Monte had been confessed to by their sons and had verified the story of the botched treasure hunt with Paul. They were going to handle the punishment of their boys a bit different than Paul. Details Paul had no interest in at this time. It was now Saturday evening and Paul took Christopher into the drawing room where they could have some privacy. This is the talk Christopher had been dreading since he escaped from Ben Bailey's yard. The time that had passed had only prolonged Christopher's agony. Paul secretly knew Christopher had learned a lesson but he also knew he had to follow through with a personal apology to Ben and return his property. It was the right thing to do. As Paul explained it to him, Christopher knew in his heart his father was right, but it still was not going to be easy for him. He was still petrified of Benjamin Bailey. He was instructed to go see Ben the next day after Church and apologize. Needless to say, Christopher did not get much sleep that night. The next morning the family rose early and Angela prepared a traditional breakfast for everyone. The Taylor's then made their way to church. Before the main service everyone would go to his or her own Sunday school. This particular Sunday, Christopher's great Aunt Eldona, and also his Sunday school teacher, just happened to have a lesson on disobeying your parents.

A Wise Teacher

Now Aunt Eldona was truly an icon in the little town of Summerville. She was Paul's Great Aunt on his mother's side of the family. She had taught Sunday school to three generations of children and had just celebrated her One Hundred Second Birthday earlier that year. Nobody in town had set so many kids on the right path of life than Aunt Eldona. She was truly a Bible Scholar and avid reader and could not resist a game of dominoes. On many occasions she would enlighten some of the young future preachers attending Seminary to some basic Bible truth when they would visit; just to pick her brain on a verse or two they did not understand. She had a great outlook on life and an unmatchable sense of humor. On many occasions someone would ask her what her secret for living a long life was and she would usually reply jokingly.

"Well, I think the secret of a long life is NOT DYING; and I prefer to look at myself as being twenty years old with eighty two years of experience." She would answer.

She would then follow up her answer with a hearty laugh and proceed to explain her real take on her life. She preferred to be called a "Seasoned Citizen" rather than a senior one."I just trust in the Lord, she would say, because I believe he has a plan for me, and when that plan is accomplished I will go and be with him for all eternity. The most important thing in this life is to give your heart and soul to him and accept him as your Savior. You have to remember, all things work together for good, to them that love him."

She would reply with unmatchable energy and a smile on her face. Even at the ripe age of one hundred and two, she was still as sharp as ever. She also had a gentle way with children and people loved to be around her.

This particular Sunday morning, Aunt Eldona could tell something was bothering Christopher. Her lesson made Christopher feel even worse for a while but then his Aunt said something that he would remember the rest of his life. "No sin is too great for God to forgive, all you have to do is confess it and tell him you are sorry and turn from it, and really mean it and he will forgive you and take your guilt away. Trust him to do it and he will." She exclaimed.

At the end of Sunday school, Aunt Eldona would always say a little prayer for the rest of the week for all of the kids in her class. But that Sunday, Christopher felt like he was the only one there and said a silent prayer himself to the Lord.

"Dear Lord, please forgive me for trespassing and stealing Mr. Bailey's property and disobeying my dad, help me to be able to do the right thing today and not be scared." Amen.

After his prayer, Christopher felt so much better. He knew it was still not going to be easy, but he felt he could go through with meeting Mr. Bailey that afternoon. Aunt Eldona noticed the change in her student and privately ask him.

"Well Mr. Christopher, are you feeling better now about your problem?" She asked.

"Yes Mam." He replied.

She bent down and gave him a big hug. "Just remember what we talked about and you will do just fine. Just trust the Lord; he will see you through anything." She said.

One evening, Aunt Eldona fell asleep while reading her Bible. This time, she would awake in heaven. She was one hundred and three years young.

Scared Stiff

After the Taylor's returned home from church and had lunch, it was time for Christopher to make his way to apologize to Ben Bailey and give him back the medal. Paul followed Christopher through the front door out to the porch.

"Are you sure you don't want me to drive you to Mr. Baileys?" Paul inquired.

"No Dad, I'll just my ride my bike, it won't take long to get there. "Christopher answered.

"Well, be careful, and remember, you'll be fine." Replied Paul.

Paul was hoping that Christopher would take him up on his ride offer if nothing else so he could be closer to

Ben's house just in case he was needed. He was also hoping that his father had made the call to alert Ben to Christopher's visit. Even though he was a little worried about his son, Paul trusted his father and knew that Christopher would be ok. He had also noticed his son had seemed to do a little growing up due to this situation. Christopher had been gone for about fifteen minutes when Paul realized Christopher had left the medal on the kitchen table. It was then Paul realized just how nervous and frightened his son must be. Maybe he had made a mistake letting him go to Ben Bailey's house alone. Paul started to panic slightly with his emotions asking himself if this was really the right way to make things good with Ben. He told Angela what was going on and he would be back later, jumped in his truck and made his way to the Bailey place. By now Christopher had arrived at Ben's house and was slowly walking up to the front lane after leaning his bike on the front dilapidated gate. The old concrete walk had giant raised cracks caused by the large tree roots that had spread from the old oak trees in the front yard, making it easy to trip if you did not watch your step. This was totally different than just passing by the old house every day to go to the swimming hole. To Christopher this was a hundred times scarier. He slowly made his way up the front steps and stopped at the front door totally petrified with fear. This seemed like the longest walk he had ever made. He could not bring himself to knock on the door. Then his eyes became fixed on Benjamin Bailey's ax he constantly carried, conveniently leaning against the front door facing; Christopher's heart felt like it was going to leap out of his chest. He decided he just could not do this. Struggling with his emotions, he turned to leave and saw his father at the end of the walk. Christopher had never been so glad to see his Dad. He ran down the walk and threw his little arms around Paul with tears streaming down his face. Paul picked up his son with a big tight hug. For a few moments neither said a word. Paul just hugged his boy tightly until he was ready to speak.

"Dad, I'm sorry, I'm too scared to see Mr. Bailey."

Paul put Christopher down and knelled to his eye level, pulled out a handkerchief and wiped his son's face.

"That's ok son, I understand more than you realize." Paul answered. "You know, I was thinking just how brave you are just coming here to apologize to Mr. Bailey, and I am so proud of you, I was wrong in making you come here by yourself, what do you say that we go talk to Mr. Bailey together, man to man?"

Christopher and Paul sat down on Ben's steps, Christopher still wiping away the salty tears.

"That would be good Dad." Christopher replied.

"Oh yeah, I almost forgot." Paul exclaimed.

Paul pulled the box with the medal inside out of his coat pocket and handed it to Christopher. "You're going to need this." Smiling as he handed the medal to Christopher.

Christopher took the medal and stuffed it in his pocket looking a little embarrassed.

"Thanks Dad."

"No problem, Paul replied, you've had a lot on your mind lately." Paul answered.

Before Paul and Christopher could make their way up the steps, the front door creaked open revealing a tall, thin weathered man standing in the doorway. The light had not revealed Ben's face yet as Christopher inched a little closer to his father's side.

"Well, I thought I heard some voices out here, can I help you two fellers?" asked Ben, as he tried to recognize the visitors.

"Are you Mr. Bailey?" Paul inquired.

"That would be me sir." Ben snapped. Paul and Christopher made their way up the rest of the steps.

"My name is Paul Taylor and this is my son Christopher." Paul explained. Paul extended his hand in which Ben returned the favor.

"You must be James's son; I must say, it's nice to finally meet you again. Why I haven't seen you since you were about the size of this little man here; that was right before I left town, seems like a hundred years ago now." Ben remarked in a slow southern drawl.

Ben bent down and extended his hand to Christopher and shook it several times. Ben's hand was so large and thin his fingers seemed to wrap around Christopher's hand more than just once. This was a pleasant change from the stern shoulder grab he had experienced a few days ago. Then Ben said something to Christopher he would never forget.

"Do you mind if I call you Chris?" Ben asked.

Now if there was anything that day that made Christopher's opinion change so quickly about Benjamin Bailey, it was that question. Only his close friends knew that he like to be called Chris. Something inside Christopher changed at that moment and he did not feel scared of Ben anymore. Maybe he wasn't such a bad man after all.

As Ben straightened up his tall frame, he gave Paul a wink and a half smile. Something also changed with Paul at that moment. This was a Benjamin Bailey he did not know, at least the image he had formed in his mind of a cantankerous old man, mad at the world never wanting to converse with anyone. Had he misjudged this man that much? With a big smile on his face and an urgent joy in his voice, Ben invited them in.

"Why don't you two fellers come in and visit for a while; I just made something in the kitchen I think you will like; especially you Chris." Ben Chuckled.

The Visit

*B*en led the way into his house with Paul and Christopher following a few steps behind. The first thing they noticed was the strong smell of paint and paint thinner in the huge main living room. The house was very old and larger than Paul's place. One could tell this had once been a magnificent mansion in its day with much history associated with it. Paul was already fascinated with the house as much as his new revelation of Ben.

Upon entering the main parlor, one had to step over all of the renovation tools Ben had been using. There were paintbrushes, rollers, rolls of new wall paper and paste and many cans of opened and unopened paint all around the room.

All of the furniture had been moved to the middle of the giant room and covered with thick drop cloths for protection.

"You fellers watch your step, as you can see I have been working on fixing up this place; I didn't realize just how much a house needs someone in it to keep it alive. It looks like I have my work cut out for me; let's just make our way back to the kitchen where it is not so cluttered so we can visit, I am due for a break anyway; I just made some chocolate chip cookies and have been letting them cool." Ben remarked.

As they followed Ben to the kitchen, Paul's thoughts were running overtime with questions he was asking himself. How was Ben ever going to finish this amount of work by himself, and this was just a few rooms, he could not imagine what repairs the upstairs rooms and the outside needed. Yes, it was obvious Ben was going to need help with this project. When they arrived at the kitchen there was a medium size oak table in the middle of the room and on it was a very large thick blue plate piled high of delicious looking chocolate chip cookies. Next to the cookies was the Gold Duster laying there in all of its glory. Ben poured Christopher a cold glass of milk while he and Paul had hot coffee. As they began to munch on the cookies, Paul couldn't help but comment.

"Mr. Bailey, these are probably the best chocolate chip cookies I have ever tasted."

Ben leaned back in his chair after finishing his bite. "Well to tell you the truth I cannot take credit, this is my mother's recipe that her mother handed down to her, they are my favorite." Ben replied chewing his cookie. "What do you think of them Chris?" Ben asked. Christopher barely managed to answer with his approval due to a mouthful full of his giant delicious cookie with the crumbs spilling onto his lap. Ben laughed at his answer and sat down and leaned back in his chair.

"Now that we are all settled, what can I do for you fellers although I have a feeling it is about this fancy treasure hunting machine?" He said, with a half grin on his face.

Paul took a sip of coffee and started the conversation Christopher had been dreading for the last few days. "Well Mr. Bailey, Christopher and I came over to." Before Paul could finish his sentence, Ben put up his hand in a stop position cutting off Paul. In a slightly stern voice he interrupted.

"First of all Paul, let's get something straight here and now." He said. "My friends call me Ben, and since you are the son of my best friend in the entire world, that's what I want you to call me."

Paul exhaled in relief. He thought Ben was angry but instantly realizing he, as well as many others in the town, had terribly misjudged Benjamin Bailey. Feeling one hundred per cent more at ease now, he started over with his apology.

"Ben, I guess you know why we are here; Christopher entered your yard without mine or your permission to look for treasure. I think it is only fitting that he apologize himself for what he did."

Paul turned and looked at Christopher and said. "Christopher, what do have to say to Ben?" Paul asked.

Christopher slowly placed the other half of his second cookie on his plate and swallowed nervously. After a slight pause he started his apology to Ben.

"Mr. Bailey." Christopher said rather timidly. Again, Ben held up his hand in the stop position but this time with a big smile across his face.

"Why don't you just call me, Mr. Ben, Chris? I like that better." Ben replied.

It was clear to Paul now; Ben Bailey had a gift for making people feel at ease. Ben knew very well what was going on and how scared Christopher had been and he was going out of his way to make his guest feel comfortable. Christopher then continued. Mr. Ben, he started, I'm very sorry I came in your yard without asking and I promise I will never do it again." He said shyly and quickly.

Ben calmly took a sip of his coffee and gently put the cup back onto the saucer and folded his hands and slightly nodded his head in approval.

"You know Chris, it was very brave for you to come here today and apologize to me, and I realize what you did was wrong but we all make mistakes."

Ben then lowered his voice slightly and leaned closer to Christopher "Now this will be just between us men but when I was young, probably around your age, I was known to have relieved some local watermelon farmers of a few choice melons myself. Now I'm not saying it was right and my father punished me but good for stealing and applied the board of education on my backside; but I learned a lesson and I think I am safe in believing you have learned a lesson out of all of this to."

Ben then raised his voice slightly. "So, my friend, apology accepted. Now have another cookie or I WILL get mad."Ben then let out a big jolly laugh.With that said, Ben rose halfway out of his chair and reached across the table and offered his hand to Christopher.

Christopher put his small hand in the middle of Ben's and they shook on it. Ben then turned his attention to the Gold Duster situated on the other half of the table."I haven't really looked at this here machine very closely; but it looks like you would have to be a rocket scientist to operate it. Sure does have a lot of gadgets and buttons on it. Maybe one day I can go with you treasure hunting and you can show me how it works." Ben asked.

Ben started to study all of the buttons and settings on the detector even more closely. "Chris, have you ever found anything valuable with this machine?" He asked.

Christopher began to answer Ben's question when he remembered the box he had found that terrible day in Ben's yard. He leaned up on one side of the large oak chair and pulled the metal box out of his back pocket. Even though the box made it uncomfortable to sit down, Christopher had almost let it slip his mind that he even had Ben's medal. Christopher handed Ben the velvet box.

"I found this in your yard that day Mr. Ben." Christopher replied. When Ben saw the box, Paul noticed an almost sad but relieved look on Ben's face. He opened the box and for a few seconds gazed at the medal as if he had been transported to another place. Paul was secretly hoping Ben would tell him about the medal but he didn't want to upset him as he could see his emotions were being stirred.

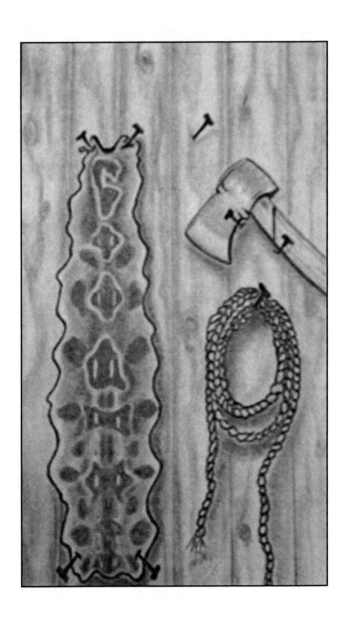

Semper Fi

The room stayed silent for a minute as Ben looked over the medal and collected his thoughts. Paul did not want to over step Ben's hospitality. He debated whether he and Christopher should say their goodbyes for the day. Then Ben leaned back in his chair slowly shaking his head from side to side began to explain."Chris, is this what you found that day in my yard by the rotten tree stump?" He questioned.

"Yes Sir, Mr. Ben." Christopher replied.

"Well Chris, I have to tell you that you are one of my heroes now; I thought I had lost my son's medal for good. I have been trying to chop up those old rotten stumps for a month now and it must have fallen out of my pocket when I was working, and now you have returned it to me."

One could tell Ben had been touched by Christopher's action and his innocence.Christopher started smiling from ear to ear; he was beginning to like Ben more and more as the evening grew longer.Paul asked. "So this is your son's medal Ben; I have to tell you when I saw what Christopher had found, I was stumped with a mystery."

Ben then started to explain to Paul. "My son was a Marine; He joined right out of college. I won't bore you with all of the specific details today, but because of his actions on a patrol he saved the lives of seven of his fellow Marines while being wounded himself very badly; wounds that never healed correctly causing him much pain later in his life. Here, I had this picture of him that was on the wall until I removed it to paint."

Ben rose and opened a large drawer and pulled out a picture of his son in his Marine uniform. Under his picture were the words SEMPER FI. He gave the picture a long look and passed it over to Paul and Christopher.

Paul looked at the picture and repeated out loud the words, SEMPER FI.

Christopher asked. What does that mean Dad?

"ALWAYS FAITHFUL." Paul stated.

"Yes and he was until the day he passed away." Ben replied solemnly. "That's where I have been these last few years, up in Virginia taking care of him. His name was Christopher also, and he liked to be called Chris, just like you do Chris." Ben glanced over at Christopher and smiled. "He was a good boy, never complained about anything even though he was in a lot of pain. One of the last things he said to me was SEMPER FI, Dad. On the day of his funeral Paul, your father showed up and stayed with me for a while. He helped me take care of Chris's affairs and convinced me to come back to this little town that I was born and raised in. One of the few things I brought back of his was his Medal of Honor. It just made me feel closer to him carrying it around with me. From now on I think I will just keep it in a safer place, at least till I get the holes sewed up in my coat pockets."

Ben looked over at Paul. "Your father has been a life-long true friend and even saved my life in the army. I'll bet you he never told you about that. To me his middle name should be SEMPER FI." Ben said.

Paul was sitting on the edge of his chair by now. The things Ben was revealing about his father were fascinating to him. These were things Paul wanted and felt like he needed to know. Paul replied to Ben's revelations. "Ben, I know it is late and we have worn out our welcome for today, but would you be willing to sit down with me from time to time and tell me about my father and your adventures in the war? My father seems hesitant to talk about much of it and if you are willing, I would be very grateful." Paul asked. Ben drew a deep breath while rubbing his thin chin.

"Sure Paul, I would be honored and would enjoy the company. I have so many stories I can tell you, you might want to write them down. You have to understand something about JB and many other guys who have experienced war, when it comes to some bad memories he rather not revisit them. But me, now, I'm a little different; it was always good to get things out; so I would be glad to talk to you. Why son, I have some war stories that will really make you grateful we live in America, and I even have some funny stories about your Dad and me and Memorial Hill. Some of these stories need to be told before they disappear. But for now, we'll just keep it between us." Ben replied.

Paul was now excited about the prospects of hearing old stories, especially from Ben, who seemed to be good at details, but when he mentioned Memorial Hill, Paul knew he would be spending a lot of time with Ben in the future with many more questions. Maybe he could help him solve the mystery of all of those exotic, colorful plants on the mysterious hill.

Paul discussed a few more details with Ben then started the good bye for now process. The three rose from the table to make their way out the front entrance when Christopher half whispered to Paul to ask about the ax. Paul then said."Ben, Christopher has one more question?" He stated while winking at Ben. "He wants to know if you were trying to chop him up with your ax that day in your yard."

Christopher slid down in his chair with total red face embarrassment. He had not planned on his father inquiring in that particular manner.

Ben got a bewildered look on his face for a moment; he then realized why Christopher was concerned. He then let out a hearty laugh realizing the origin of the question."Why don't you fellers follow me and I will clear up your concerns.This is something you will have to see to believe." Ben said between chuckles. Ben lead them out of the kitchen door to the back covered porch and pointed to the wall still chuckling at Christopher's question. There nailed to the wall was the largest rattlesnake skin Paul had ever seen.

"That old boy was coiled and ready to strike you, Chris." Ben explained. "It's a good thing I had my ole trusty ax because if he had bitten you, I'm not sure you would have made it. He was full of poison. When I was a boy, one of these reptiles bit my dog and killed it, and my dog weighed more than you do soaking wet, and that snake wasn't nearly as big as this ole boy. Sorry I scared you, but you boys didn't stick around too long for any explanations." Ben chuckled.

Ben then turned to Paul, who was pale and speechless thinking about what Ben had just revealed.

"I've never seen anybody run as fast as those three young ons, now I know why." Ben laughed heartedly. Ben continued explaining in his deep story telling voice as if he was making an important speech in front of a large crowd."Yep, I was cleaning a window when I saw three Ninja like figures sneaking through my fence. I was getting a kick out of watching them when I noticed this Ole Boy."

Ben pointed to the snake skin.

"He was making a beeline for Chris. I don't think I have ever seen one move that fast, and it was obvious

he had a mission and was highly disturbed by something. Well sir, I grabbed my ax, and thank the Good
Lord my aim was good that day cause he was rattling
that old tail so fast you could have heard it in the next
county; only Chris here had those muffs on his ears
and couldn't hear a thing. That old devil was coiled and
ready to strike when I whacked his head clean off just
before he made his leap at young Chris here's neck."

Ben took another gulp of coffee then continued. "I
guess when I moved out, these rattlers figured they
would just move in and take over the place. For some
reason they like my yard and I have been trying to run
them off since I came back. Too bad they don't have
hands or I'd put a paintbrush in them and put em to
work. Why, I'd be finished fixin this old place up in no
time. That's the reason I have those no trespassing
signs up, so nobody will get bit. Maybe I should put up
a BEWARE OF SNAKES warning on them also." Ben
finished.

Paul had developed such a sick feeling inside, realizing what could have happened to Christopher, that he only heard half of Ben's explanation. It was very clear to a very grateful father; Benjamin Bailey has saved his only sons life.

Sunday Evening

The afternoon was quickly turning into evening so Paul and Christopher said their goodbyes to Ben with the understanding that Paul would be visiting whenever possible in the near future. Ben wrapped up some extra Chocolate Chip cookies and sent them to Angela, Arielle and Alyssa by Christopher with a friendly warning not to eat them before getting home. Paul loaded Christopher's bike in the back of the truck and they rode home together. The two were about half way home when Paul started to talk about their visit."You know son, I am really ashamed of myself." Paul confessed. Christopher turned to his father with a puzzled look.

"Why are you ashamed Dad?" He questioned.

Paul hesitated for a moment as he straightened up the truck after turning a sharp curve.

"Well Son, all this time I have been prejudging Mr. Bailey thinking he was something he wasn't."

Christopher looked puzzled. "What do you mean Dad?" He quizzed.

"I thought that Mr. Bailey was a grouchy old man that didn't want anyone to bother him and he was just mad at the world and didn't like anybody or anything; turns out he is not that at all, even the no trespassing signs were put there for our protection more than his. Yes, I have truly misjudged him and I feel bad about it; I am just thankful we have met the real Benjamin Bailey now; I guess that will teach me a life lesson of not to prejudge people from now on." Paul said.

Christopher turned and looked out the passenger window and was silent for a moment in little boy thought. He then turned to his father.

"Dad, it teaches me a lesson too." He said.

Paul glanced over to his son. "I'm glad you realize that son, it shows you are growing up." Paul replied. After agreeing on their mistake, they also realized they had made a new friend in Benjamin Bailey; a very good friend. Paul started thinking how he could somehow repay Ben for saving Christopher from the rattler. He had also planned to discuss the lost gold situation with Ben, but now he felt there were other things that needed attention before any hunting for gold would occur. He was going to have to be careful how he would explain the incident to Angela without her totally coming unglued at the prospects of what could have happened to their son.

Angela was anxiously relaxing on the porch swing waiting for them to return and was glad to see the smiles on their faces as they approached the house. After giving them a big hug she told Paul she could not wait to hear the details of their visit with Ben. Upon getting settled and eating supper Paul and Angela sent the kids up to their rooms so they could talk privately. Paul explained every detail of the successful visit without leaving out a single fact. Angela took the snake story fairly well but Paul could tell she was upset and was trying to hide it."I know it is hard to relive the incident but we just have to be thankful Ben was there to save Christopher." Paul exclaimed.

"I know honey but it is so hard to think of what could have happened. I can't wait to meet Mr. Bailey in person to thank him, if fact even before I do that, I am going to sit down tonight and write him a thank you note and invite him over for a good home cooked meal. You know Paul; I think we need to try to do something even more special for Mr. Bailey." Angela added.

Paul's interest was peaking now, as he could not wait to tell Angela what his idea was to help out with Ben's renovation project."You know Angela; funny you should mention that, I was just telling Christopher those same thoughts on the way home. What do you think of getting a few good carpenters and painters around town to help Ben out with repairing his house; you know, just like Aunt Evelyn did for us when we came back home.

I'll never forget that day and the great feeling I had when I saw what the town had done for us." Paul said.

"Neither will I Paul that was one of the best days of my life. That was a gift and memory that will keep on giving for life." Angela answered.

Paul could tell the wheels of Angela's mind had been set into motion.

"Paul, I think it's a great idea, and I can spread the word to the ladies in town to help also, I'm sure from the way you described his house it is going to need a little bit of a woman's touch also." Angela commented.

"Oh I think it is going to need a touch from just about everyone in town to get that placed fixed up." Paul added. The couple laughed and agreed to start planning for the project the next day.

Later that night when Paul and Angela had tucked in Alyssa and Arielle, they purposefully saved Christopher for last just to double check on him. After his prayers he asked Paul and Angela if he could tell his friends about Ben and what he had done for him."I think that is a great idea, Christopher; people should know what kind of man Ben really is." Paul exclaimed.

Angela agreed, they then told Christopher their plans to help Ben. Even he was excited about helping his new friend fix up his home.

"Maybe I can get some of my friends to help too." Christopher said.

"I think that would be a very good thing to do son; we can use all the man and women power we can get on this project, and your mother and I thank you for offering." Paul exclaimed. Angela pulled the covers up over her son and tucked him in for the night.

"Now, young man, you get a good night sleep; you've had a long day and I think you need a good rest; especially tonight." Angela said.

"Yes mom." He answered. Paul and Angela kissed him goodnight.

As they made their way back downstairs, Angela took Paul's hand and said. "You know honey, we have some great kids."

Paul pulled her small hand up and kissed it. "Yes Sweetheart, we sure do, and thanks to the good Lord and Ben Bailey, they are all accounted for and safe tonight."

Organizing

*P*aul started the week planning the details of Ben's house renovation. He talked to his father and many other key people in Summerville that could lend a hand on the project. Everyone thought it was a great idea and were eager to help and it didn't hurt that the story of the rattlesnake incident was starting to circulate around the town. Ben was becoming a town hero. Paul wanted to be sure to have everything finished before the winter set in. He had noticed that Ben's roof was in bad repair so that would be the place to start. It took a few days to procure all of the materials, still the planning went smoothly. Paul was more concerned if Ben would accept the gift that the town wanted to give him but he was ready to pull in some heavy hitters to convince him if he was hesitant to cooperate. Paul was a salesman and he was confident he could sell Ben on the idea.

Ben accepted Angela's invitation to supper the next week and he and the Taylor's had a great time together. It was only the first of many as he was invited to every holiday get together the Taylor's had. Ben was a true gentleman and enjoyed the company of the family. Paul, Angela and Ben had a nice talk after dinner and Ben was overwhelmed when they told him what the town wanted to do for him.

"So Ben, it's settled." Paul said, while grinning from ear to ear. "We will start immediately starting from the top of the roof to the bottom of the root cellar."

"This is truly an answer to my prayers." Ben replied very humbly."It is really hard to find anyone, especially this time of year that has time to do repairs and to say my place only needs repairs is a giant understatement.Folks, I can't tell you how I appreciate this, I was preparing to go to the hardware store and buy out all of the buckets just to catch the rain from that leaky roof." Ben chuckled. "It will be the town's way of welcoming you home and getting reacquainted with you; I can't wait to get to work." Paul exclaimed.

Ben visited a few more minutes and graciously thanked everyone; especially Angela for her home cooked meal and kind thank you note. Before he left, Angela gave him the biggest thank you hug she could muster. The Taylor's could tell he was looking forward to the next few weeks of renovating but even more of socializing and getting to know the town's people he had been separated from so long. Paul and Angela went back into the house after walking Ben out. "You know, Angela, I just thought of something that is very sad." Paul said.

Angela looked puzzled at Paul's statement. "What's that honey?" She inquired.

"According to Dad, Ben really has no family left." He answered.

Angela paused for a few seconds, then turned and gave Paul a hug. "Yes he does, we are his new family now."

Paint Up, Fix Up And Just Visiting

*I*n only a few days the town's best Roofers, Painters and Carpenters were showing up early at Ben's place. Paul got great pleasure in the excitement and enthusiasm the people were exhibiting with the project. It was like an old fashion barn rising. Before long, work started both inside and outside on the huge mansion. The ladies of the town started working on the inside details of restoring wall paper and some painting. Even Sam and Monte joined Christopher in painting the massive porch. Sam and Monte also apologized, in their own boyish way to Ben for trespassing after some stern prodding from their fathers. But they also grew just as fond of Ben as the rest of the town. Ben supplied the daily picnic style lunches with the ladies help and it seemed his chocolate chip cookies became a hit with the whole town. Ben made it a point to talk to and really get to know all of the people who were so graciously spending their time to help him. Of course, everyone had to hear the famous rattlesnake story and look at the skin on the back porch again and again, especially the younger boys. Paul noticed Ben would almost get embarrassed when asked to tell the story as he did not think he had really done that much; but Paul knew better. Even a few more rattlers were chased off the grounds as the work was being completed. Ben would make the people laugh when he said the snakes seemed to think they had "squatter's rights "to his yard. Then the grown-ups would have to explain what that term meant to the kids.

With the cooperation of the weather, it only took a few weeks of hard work to bring the old place back to its glory days of beauty and newness. Everyone was happy that they were able to complete all of the outside repairs before the winter would set in with the snow. After the work was completed, Ben had an open house party in his "community project" as he called it, for the people of the town. Everyone and anyone were invited and it was a memorable event. Angela had the military picture of Ben's son beautifully reframed in her shop and added his Congressional Medal of Honor under his image with the words SEMPER FI in gold letters. She presented it to Ben as a house warming gift from the town. It was strategically hung in the huge main library room near the folded American flag that was draped over his son's casket then presented to Ben by the Marine Corps. The flag and picture were place in the room where Ben would see it every day. Ben was brought to tears when he saw it and compensated by making the joke that even he could never lose it again with it hanging on the wall. He then warmly and gra-ciously thanked everyone for their kindness and hard work and made it clear his home would always be their home also.

After the homecoming celebration and in the years that followed, Ben once again became one of Summerville's greatest assets. He no longer was viewed as a hermit or feared by the younger children or even criticized by the town's people. He became very involved with the people and all of the events of the town. He always wore a big smile on his face and was always there for his fellow man. The town grew to love Benjamin Bailey. Paul had accomplished his mission. Now the town also knew, Benjamin Bailey was a good man, a good friend, and back to his home town to stay.

Fall

*F*all was slowly starting to give warnings of its beautiful arrival to Summerville. The air was crisp and the leaves would turn colors that didn't have a proper name to describe their beauty. The chilly weather had silenced the evening symphony of insects, bullfrogs and Whippoorwills. Fall had arrived and it was Paul's favorite time of year. It was also a busy but fun time of year for everyone in the town. Harvest time was here; the fall festivals and county fairs were the events everyone looked forward to. This year would turn out to be one of the best county fairs ever for Summerville. Everyone had something to contribute. There were prizes for the biggest pumpkins, best looking livestock of every kind and the variety of food aromas would keep you hungry the whole daylong. Angela entered some of her shadowboxes and framing and won first prize, while Aunt Evelyn picked up a few ribbons herself for her chow-chow and her cornbread recipe. The local ladies club quilting sessions had also produced some beautiful blue ribbon results. JB Taylor and Ben Bailey were in charge of the hayrides for the kids while Paul and Walton helped with the administration end of the plan. All in all it was a time to store in your memories of good things, a time that would never repeat itself in the same manner at the same time, ever again.

History

*A*fter the fall festivals and the fairs were history for the year, things would slow down a little before the official holiday season. Paul and Christopher still had the stolen gold on their minds even though they hadn't discussed it much. Paul just could not find the proper time to sit down with Ben and tell him the story and show him the documents he had discovered.

One fall afternoon Paul stopped by Ben's house just to see how he was doing. Ben liked to take a break and visit anytime with Paul. He loved talking about old times and history. This particular afternoon Ben was full of stories of his and JB Taylor's younger days. Paul had wanted to hear about the war days from Ben for many months now, and it seemed this day Ben was hit with the urge to tell one of his favorites.

"Paul, I'll bet your father never told you about the time he saved my life in the army." Ben inquired.

Paul eagerly answered. "No he hasn't Ben, but I would like to hear any story you can tell me about you and my father."

Ben continued. "Well Paul, your father and I left on the same train that day along with thirteen other teenagers to go to California for basic training. We were training for a top-secret mission that we didn't even know about until after it happened. Anyway, part of the training was landing on the beaches of California for practice. Well sir, JB and I were on the same landing craft and almost into shore when a giant wave came out of nowhere and actually tipped us over. Now you can ask your dad, but he knows I am more of a fisherman than a fish and I was swallowing more water than any fish my size and had pretty much decided I was a goner when I felt this hand grab my pack belt and pull me up to the top. I was upchucking water for who knows how long and when I finally got back to my senses and could see straight I saw your father's mug looking down at me asking me if I was all right. So, you see son, your father saved my life, although he won't talk about it himself. Yes sir, he pretty much looked after me till we were separated into different units, then for a while we lost touch. When the war ended and we came home, we arrived in town about two weeks apart. We met up after that and found out a few weeks later that out of the fifteen guys who left that day on the train, your father and I were the only two that made it back alive. After we heard that news, we didn't see each other for a little while, I don't know if it was just getting back in the routine of life or we were just trying to put the war behind us. Maybe it was just a little of both."

Ben stopped for a few moments as if he were reliving his story and maybe thinking about the soldiers that didn't return. It was getting late and Paul thought it might be good time to take his leave for now. After a few questions on some details of the story, Ben told Paul to come back the next day and he would tell him a secret about Memorial Hill, that is, if he could first get permission from someone to tell the story. This peaked Paul's interest like nothing else could. "What time can I come back tomorrow?" Paul asked, with the excitement of a young child with a new toy.

"If you can, come by right after lunch so we can talk longer." Ben answered. Paul did not know what Ben had in mind for the next day's meeting, all he knew was he had been trying to find out the real story where the colorful and exotic plants had come from growing on Memorial Hill for years, and his intuitions told him Ben had some information stored in his fertile brain that he wanted to advertise. Needless to say, Paul could hardly sleep that night due to looking forward to the next Benjamin Bailey story.

A Mystery Revealed

The next day Paul rose early and got his morning chores completed half time to go back to Ben's house and hear the story of Memorial Hill. To Paul, it was almost as exciting as Christmas mornings when he was younger to hear stories and discover the real history that happened in his little town. He had a good feeling about this meeting and remembered to take his pencils and tablet to write details of the stories down. After lunch Paul made his way back to Ben's house. When he arrived and reached the front gate, he was surprised to see his father sitting with Ben on the porch rocking in the large oak rocking chairs, just rocking and talking and laughing. Paul stopped for a few seconds just to get a mental picture of the two lifelong friends exchanging conversation. He could only imagine what a wealth of adventures these two warriors had experienced in their life and he was hoping to hear about them for many meetings to come. He would come to find out over the next few months just how surviving a terrible war had galvanized their friendship forever. It was a bond that had lasted from early childhood to their senior years and had never wavered. Paul walked up the lane to the porch and greeted his father and Ben. They seemed very glad to see him and both were in a particular jolly mood.

"Did I interrupt an important meeting?" Paul exclaimed.

"Not at all." Ben replied. "Your dad and I were just visiting the past, wondering where the years had gone. You'll be doing the same one day." Both men chuckled. "I am beginning to already know what you mean; time seems to be flying by faster every day." Paul replied, while shaking his head in agreement.

After a few more minutes of small talk, Ben started to explain why he had JB Taylor drop by to help him with his story. Ben just jumped right into his story almost before Paul could get comfortable in his own rocking chair.

"You see Paul, what I am about to tell you has been a mystery and a secret in this town since your father and I came back from the war; and we are the only two people who know the real story of why Memorial Hill is so beautiful, and we made a promised to each other that we would get each other's permission before we could ever reveal the secret. Your father and I figured since we are no longer spring chickens and the story must live on, so we have decided to let you in on the "truth of the hill" as we call it."

Now Paul knew Ben had a way with words and he loved to tell a story, so he was trying to figure out if Ben was maybe adding a little sensationalism to the whole thing. He looked over at his father, who was just rocking and smiling in silent agreement with Ben's statement.

"OK Ben, my pencil is sharp and my paper is clean and I am ready to hear "The story of the hill." Paul replied.

Ben leaned back in the old rocking chair and started his story just as if he might be reciting a speech to run for some political office. Paul noticed even Ben's voice would seem to change. He had an uncanny way of taking you with him and opening up your imagination as if you were watching a movie. Yes, Ben surely had the gift of storytelling.

"I guess if you want to know the complete story of the hill, I will have to start way back at the beginning of my time in the war." Ben declared.

"After your Dad and I were assigned to different units it was not long till some of the upper officer's found out I was a fairly good shot and loved to hunt back home. They decided to take advantage of these talents and strongly suggested I become somewhat of a scout for them. It was explained to me that my mission would be to strike out before our unit and stay around a mile or two ahead and report back with any enemy activity. Let me tell you, after I started this scouting stuff, I was so tired at the end of the day, I never had a problem sleeping anywhere, even if we were being shelled all night. Some of the guys started calling me Rip Van Bailey, but that is another story for another time." Ben said hesitating for a few seconds."Well, one day I was out scouting for machine gun nest that would give us some trouble advancing. I had located about three of them and to my knowledge I had not been discovered. Also, to my knowledge I did not realize the Germans had placed a sniper in a strategic position in a tree not far away. Well sir, I had just filled my canteen from a local stream and put my Chlorine pill in it to kill any germs in that nasty stream water. Some of my buddies hated the taste that pill would create but I loved it because it killed those stomach bug critters."

Paul laughed to himself silently as Benjamin Bailey was very thorough in his stories and did not leave out any details even the smallest ones. Ben continued his story.

"I had crawled up through some grass I thought was hiding me pretty good. I had my binoculars and had spied the enemy's nest, three to be exact. As I scanned the hills and trees, I came across a sniper in a tree who spotted me about the same time as I had him and he was training his sites on me. As soon as I spotted him and knowing he was going to shoot me the first chance he got, I started rolling back and forth with bullets kicking up the dirt around me."

Ben started laughing. "It must had frustrated that sniper to death, he probably never saw anyone just commence to rolling back and forth like that and that could have been a factor that saved my life. After he fired around five rounds, I got up and started running and zig- zagging through the half open field. Then to make matters worse, one of the machine gun nest spotted me and decided to give me some machine gun dancing lessons in that field. Paul that day I could have out danced Fred Astaire and Gene Kelly combined and I had not run so fast since I played high school football going for that winning touchdown, but I made it to a group of large trees and took cover to catch my breath. Then, I felt something wet on my leg and immediately thought I had been shot and was bleeding. As I frantically searched for a wound, all the time wondering why I had not felt any pain, I discovered one of the snipers bullets had hit my full canteen that had soaked my leg. A bullet fragment had somehow been caught in the canteen and had not exited and was still rattling around in there, which, by the way I still to this day consider a miracle. I started to throw it away but something told me to keep it, in case nobody would believe my story. My commanding officer later told me my information help save many lives that day. Now, Paul I bet you are wondering what in heavens name this has to do with Memorial Hill?" Ben quizzed raising his eyebrows.

Not giving Paul a second to respond, Ben continued the story. "So, listen carefully, and I will tell you."Ben then leaned back in the old rocking chair and started to slightly rock back and forth to finish his story ."Son, for some reason, I kept that canteen for the rest of the war, stuffed a piece of cork in the hole and at every little village and town our unit would go through, if there were any flower seeds, plant bulbs or anything else that was beautiful growing, I would take a few and put them in that lifesaving canteen; when nobody was looking of course. I thought maybe my mother would like to plant them if I made it back home and it would brighten up the old home place. To tell you the truth, I really did not know for a long time why I did that, until I got back home. I think by carrying it around with me it just helped remind me of home and my folks, a silly private, reason to live through that war. Now, this is where your dad here comes into the picture."

Ben looked over at James Taylor and gave him a wink and a nodding smile, which was instantly returned. Paul would noticed his father's eyes while Ben was telling his story. It was almost like he was in pain and happy at the same time. Many times his smile did not match the sadness in his eyes; it was like looking at two separate faces. Paul surmised his father was remembering things about the war that were not a pleasant revisit; trying to separate his past experiences with his life now and how it had turned out. At that point Paul's love and respect for his father and Ben was heightened and he wanted to say something to both of them; but he could find no words that he thought would be sufficient. After Ben took a slight rest; he proceeded with his story.

"Your dad and I returned from the war around two weeks from each other. I got back here first, then JB. It was just a few weeks when we got together for the first time and learned that out of fifteen guys who left on that train that day headed for boot camp, only your father and I came home alive. In fact we shared our thoughts on that subject right here on this very porch so many years ago. We both gave it some time to try to forget a lot of horrible things we saw and the experiences we had; some were good, but most of them were tragic. My

191

Captain used to say; "If you want to survive in this war, a part of you will have to die inside." "At first I did not know what he meant; after a few battles it was clear to me what he was saying; but I tried my best to not let it change me. A lot of people use to call us heroes but every soldier that came home knew the real heroes were the guys that did not make it back home." Ben paused for a moment. "Yes, those are the real heroes in war."

Ben then paused and didn't say anything else for what seemed like an hour even though in reality it was only a few seconds. He stopped rocking and put one of his hands on the bottom of his chin and began to rub it back and forth. He then began to speak again."It is very hard to explain Paul, but both your dad and I felt kind of guilty because we were blessed enough to return home in one piece and we talked about it a lot, just him and me. One day many years ago we were talking and telling war stories and I told him the same one I'm telling you today. Well, I went back into my stuff and found that canteen still full of flower seeds and such. Then your father came up with a brilliant idea for us to plant everything in that canteen on Memorial Hill in honor of our fallen brothers. We waited until the brightest full moon one night, so we could see and not be seen and planted the whole canteen full of seeds and bulbs at the top of the hill. Then I buried the canteen up there on the hill with the bullet still rattling inside it. We didn't know if anything would ever grow, and for a while it didn't. Then one spring, that hill just busted out all over with every unusual plants and colors you could imagine, and over the years it has spread all over the hill; just the way it is today." Ben exclaimed.

"Why did you not want anyone to see you?" Paul interjected."Well, in those days we would have been considered sissies if anyone found we were planting flowers in the moonlight." Ben answered.

James Taylor quickly quipped; "Now he just bakes sissy chocolate chip cookies every other day; isn't it funny how times change?" Ben quickly responded to his friend's barb. "I seem to recall the last batch of "sissy"cookies I made disappeared into your oversized belly fairly quickly with no complaints." Ben stated.

Ben kept rocking in his chair trying hard to suppress a full fledge laugh waiting for his friends response. Paul looked over to his father for a reply. He to was trying hard not to laugh and just replied with. "Point taken Ben."

His father then winked at Paul as if to say; "Mission accomplished."All three then had a good laugh before Ben finished the story. Ben leaned back in his rocking chair once again to continue.

"Now back to the story I was telling before I was so ruuuudely interrupted." Ben said in jest.

"So after we accomplished our secret mission on the hill, your father and I then made a promise to each other, a promise that has held true until today, that we would keep the secret of Memorial Hill between just us. We even took trips to visit the families of our fallen brothers. We would see if we could help the families with any work like fixing their old tractor or even helping them plant their crops. We didn't want any credit or pay and refused it when offered. In fact you're the first person we have admitted this to. It was just our way of honoring our brothers that did not make it home. So, that is the truth of the matter, as JB here is my witness. Now we are passing it to you to do whatever you want with it." Ben finished.

Paul then realized the reason on many occasions he would visit his father he noticed him staring out of his window at Memorial Hill with a peaceful gaze that defied explanation. He was reminiscing about the past. Their amazing story had answered all of Paul's questions. Paul asked a few more questions of the men and thanked them for everything more than once. He was finally unlocking some of the mysteries of Summerville that he had thought about for years. Paul, JB, and Ben would meet many more times and Paul would record many more stories. With every story he would gain more and more respect for the sacrifice that had been made from ordinary people who fought and died for America's and the world's freedom.

Paul liked to use the old fashion number two lead pencils to write the history Ben revealed and he must have used a case of them while recording Ben's stories; like the other sniper bullet that found it's mark square in the front of Ben's helmet and instead of killing him it tumbled over the top of the inside of the helmet and exited out the rear; or the story of how Ben had climbed up in a church bell tower to do some sniping himself and ran out of ammo; one minute later after he had climbed down to attain more ammo an undetected enemy tank blew up the top of the tower just before Ben was to climb back up. Every time Ben revealed one of these incidences, Paul would notice he would sometimes randomly stop in the middle of the story and reflect. Paul did not realize it but after all of these years Benjamin Bailey was realizing God had been protecting him all of his life and still had a plan for him.

Warm Holidays

The holiday season had arrived in the little town of Summerville. Everyone seemed to love this season of the year and even though there were many more things going on in everyone's life, time seemed to slow down to a more relaxing pace. Paul's business did not require him to travel that often from Thanksgiving to the New Year, so he had more time to spend with Angela and the kids, however Angela's shop was doing a thriving business and Christmastime was busy for her. Still, she was very involved in all of the hustle and bustle of the extra activities going on in town and with their church. The first snow fell in November just before Thanksgiving and the children of the town could hardly wait for the Christmas vacation to come where school was just a memory for a few fun filled days. With snow and a hard winter freeze, the hills would come alive with every variety of sled known to man to run the hills, some even homemade. When not sleighing down the slopes, one could expect to find everyone ice skating on the shallow pond at the end of town. Paul and Angela would stand on the porch and watch all of the different color wool hats racing down the hills with Christopher, Arielle and Alyssa square in the middle of the fun.The Taylor's would always have the family and friends over for the holiday dinners and parties and Benjamin Bailey always had a standing invitation. Ben had a large old antique sleigh he renovated and would break it out just after the first snowfall and a hard freeze sealed the earth for winter. All of the kids and even some adults of the town loved to ride in it. If it was packed right, it could hold a bundle of passengers, as it was larger than your average sleigh. Ben used the sleigh even more than he used his truck this time of year. He also used it to deliver food baskets and other needed items to needy families near the town. James Taylor had established the program years ago and since Ben had returned to Summerville he had drafted his more than willing friend to help him.

Even though it was a busy time, Paul was planning to talk to Ben about getting permission to hunt for the stagecoach gold when the weather would permit it. He wanted plenty of uninterrupted time to tell him what he had discovered and show him the documents he had uncovered in the secret room. He planned on maybe a day right after Christmas when things had slowed down a little. He also wanted Christopher to be involved as much as possible as Ben and Christopher had become very close since that summer. Paul was a bit concerned on how Ben might take the news that one of his ancestors had robbed the stage, even though it was over a hundred years ago, but he was going to take that chance anyway. Ben seemed to have a very good nature and Paul had never seen him angry, besides, maybe he might have some documentation himself on his famous mysterious relative; the infamous Samuel Bailey

Fil And Mil

$\mathcal{W}$hen Paul first met Angela, he quickly became aware that when they were married he got a special bonus package deal with her parents. Although they lived in a large city far from the rural Summerville town, Paul's in laws came to visit as much as possible. Usually, it was about twice a year, once in the spring and at Christmas time. Paul did not feel comfortable calling them by their first names and he could not explain why, so the three got together and came up with the nicknames of FIL, which was short for Father-in-law, and MIL, just for laughs, was the short version of Mother-in-law. Paul's nickname was SIL for Son-in-law. Paul's in laws were two of the nicest and giving people he had ever known with Fil and Mil being the life of the party. Their favorite time of the year seemed to be, anytime of the year. When visiting over the years, Fil and Mil had developed many good friends in town, and would often refer to Summerville as their second home. Family was everything to the two and they helped Paul and Angela any way they could. A visit from them would always cheer up Angela when she would get homesick and they always managed to be there no matter what obstacle would present itself, especially when all three of the grand babies were born. Fil was quite the wood worker and would always leave something behind for the kids he had hand crafted from his woodworking shop. The Taylor's had quite a collection of reminders of them all year long. Fil could make anything out of a block of wood. When Christmas, then spring approached, half of the town would be inquiring when the In-laws would be arriving. Paul would often hound them trying to convince them to move to Summerville and would always receive an answer of "well you just never know." Still, everyone in the family and the town agreed, it just would not be a complete year unless there were a few visits from Fil and Mil.

A Christmas Eve To Remember

Christmas Eve had finally come to Summerville and everyone in the Taylor house was healthy, happy and excited this special night. There was a tradition in the Taylor home to have a feast on Christmas Eve with an open invitation to all friends and family to stop by and visit, eat and just relax in front of the roaring fire. It was one of the best memories Paul and Angela would carry forward. Many times, relatives and old friends that had long moved away would come back just to visit with high hopes of running into an old classmate or friend. The party had also been responsible for a couple of marriages when long lost high school sweethearts would meet by chance. The old mansion had plenty of room to accommodate all of the bodies that showed up. Paul and Angela would get an extra dose of Christmas spirit that day, especially when people would tell them that the holiday would not be complete without their party. It was the perfect ending to every year whether the year had been good or challenging. It was fun to see how the families would grow and change from year to year.

Late that afternoon just before sunset the day was slowing down a bit. The entire group of guest had left except Paul's parents. Paul was out gathering more firewood when Ben Bailey rode up in his sleigh. Ben had somehow found the perfect new horse to pull his newly renovated sleigh. The animal was much larger than a regular size horse and was more than capable of towing many people in the giant red sleigh. As Ben pulled up the drive he did his Santa imitation hoping Paul's family, especially the kids would hear him.Whoooooah Boy, Whoooooaaah, Merrrrrrry Christmas everyone. Merrrrry

Christmas. Ben belted out. Then he finished up with a big HO HO HO.

"Well, Merry Christmas to you, Santa Ben." Paul answered. "I was wondering if you were going to make it today, and where did you get this beautiful animal?" Paul inquired.

Ben jumped out of the sleigh and tied the horse to one of the porch support pillars.

"Well Paul, I was coming home one day last week from Oakville and passed this little farm and saw this big fellow out in the pasture. Now don't ask me why because I can't explain it but I went and ask the old farmer that owned him if he would sell him, well Sir, as you can see we reached an agreement and you are looking at "Traveler", probably the smartest horse I have ever owned. You know Paul, I don't know much about a lot of things, but I do know a good piece of horse flesh when I see it and I could tell this ole fellow was not ready for retirement. He loves to pull this sleigh and is a big showoff." Ben answered.

Paul walked around Traveler while patting him on his firm neck. The horse was much larger than your average horse. He looked like a cross between a Morgan and a Clydesdale. Even with his size he still had a gentle look in his eyes. Traveler would always hold his head high making it difficult for even a taller than average man to bridle him.

"Ben, he is one fine steed; I can't wait for the kids to see him." Paul said.

Ben pulled a few sugar cubes out of his pocket and fed them to Traveler then made his way to the back of the sleigh chocked full of presents.

"Paul, I wouldn't miss visiting you guys for the world, especially on Christmas Eve. Come help me with these boxes of presents, and be very careful with it as there are some breakables in there." Ben warned.

Paul grabbed one of the boxes and escorted Ben into the house where everyone was relaxing by the fire in the drawing room. After the greetings Ben proceeded to explain his visit. "Folks, I am in the Christmas Spirit tonight. I haven't felt like this in a long time and I want to show my appreciation to all of you. I know these gifts are not much but they are given from my heart and I hope you will like them."

Angela stepped up to Ben and kissed him on the cheek wishing him a Merry Christmas putting a hot cup of apple cider in his weathered hands.

"Ben, you did not have to give us gifts, by you just being here with us makes Christmas complete." She answered gently.

To hide his emotion, Ben quickly jumped to the subject of the gifts again. "Well, they're not much, but I hope you and the little ones will like them." He answered.

With that said, he began to carefully rummage through the box just like Santa, first pulling out two dolls, one for Arielle and one for Alyssa. Angela immediately picked up on the fact that these were not just ordinary dolls; they were the most beautiful and well preserved antique dolls she had ever seen. Ben gave each of the girls a doll and started to explain."You know, I have been going through old trunks and boxes in the attic, and one day I came across these young ladies wrapped in a cheese cloth and stored in their own cedar box along with their little dresses. I couldn't believe how good they look after all of these years. I believe they belonged to my Grandmother."

Ben kneeled down on one knee to get closer to the little girls.

"But you know, they didn't look happy because they didn't have their own little girl to take care of them, so the first two little girls I thought of to give them a home, were you two, and I think these little ladies are way overdue for someone to love and take care of them.

"Both Arielle and Alyssa had already started to cuddle the dolls like a newborn baby. "This is the most beautiful dolly I have ever seen." Arielle exclaimed.

"My dolly looks like a real little girl." Alyssa added.

"And, I also have a whole trunk of clothes I found for them." Ben added.

Angela told Ben she would explain to the girls how fragile and special the dolls were and how to take good care of them. Arielle and Alyssa gave Ben a big hug and said thank you almost in unison, something they did quite often. Ben informed Angela he had also found two miniature doll trunks full of old handmade doll clothes he would bring over to the girls in the coming days.

Ben went back to the box on the table and pulled out three more wrapped boxes. "I'm not finished yet, these two go to two special men and this one goes to Angie." Ben handed Angela, Paul, and Christopher each a gift.

"Open yours first Mom." Exclaimed Christopher.

"Well, alright, don't mind if I do." Angela answered.

Angela unwrapped a copy of Ben's mother's secret Chocolate Chip recipe he had had beautifully hand stitched and framed for her to hang in her kitchen.

"Ben, this is beautiful but it is your secret recipe, are you sure you want me to.

Ben politely interrupted. "Yes, I'm very sure I want you to have it. I know you will do my chocolate chip cookies justice and they will probably be better than any I ever baked. Please, take it and enjoy."

"Ben this is so nice of you, I know exactly where I am going to put it. But I am curious, where did you have this framed?" She asked.

"Well, it wasn't easy as it was done right in your little shop by your co-worker, Bobi Stone. I found out she is famous for her framing work and needlepoint. How she pulled it off and kept it a secret is beyond me, especially when you are working beside her every day." Ben replied chuckling.

Angela laughed. "That's amazing; you two really did pull it off and she did a beautiful job on the framing. I bet she did it while I was working at the Library in the afternoons. Thank you Ben, I will always cherish this." Angela gave Ben a big hug. Everyone then turned to Paul and Christopher to watch them open their gifts. They opened them up the same time revealing a beautiful snakeskin wallet with Christopher's slightly smaller than Paul's. Christopher was the first to react.

"Wow, Mr. Ben, this is neat."

Yes Ben, these are beautiful wallets." Paul added.

"Do you fellers recognize anything familiar about those money holders yet?" Ben asked.

Paul looked puzzled for a few seconds then realized what Ben was talking about.

"Is this what I think it is Ben, or maybe I should ask WHO I think it is?" Paul exclaimed. Before Ben could answer, Christopher chimed in. "This is the snake that almost bit me." He cried.

Ben threw back his head in laughter, and in his southern drawl answered. "You guessed it Chris, that's what's left of the old boy that tried to take you out last summer. I figured I would make good use of his old carcass and make something nice for you and your Dad. It seemed a shame to let that skin go to waste, but I have to tell ya, it wasn't easy, that old devil was tough. But I think he turned out a couple of pretty good money hiders; don't you?" Ben was still laughing at their reaction.

Paul and Christopher were too busy examining their new wallets to react to Ben's laughter.

"So guys, what do you think?" Ben quizzed.

"I think it is one of the neatest gifts ever, wait till the guys see this; thanks Mr. Ben." Christopher beamed.

Ben continued. "The great thing about those wallets is there is a story behind them, and that is the kind of gifts I like to give. It marked the beginning of a great friendship that I will always cherish."

"So will we Ben." Angela added.

Paul had gone into the other room for a few minutes and came out with a large box almost half as tall as himself.

"We didn't forget you this Christmas Ben." Paul exclaimed.

Paul set the box down near Ben. "Merry Christmas, Ben." Paul said smiling ear to ear.

As he took the top off of the box Ben got a big smile on his face. "You folks did not have to do this; you sure know how to make a feller feel Christmassy." Ben replied.

In the box was a wide leather harness with giant jingle bells securely fastened all over the belt designed to strap on the horse while pulling a sleigh. Paul and Angela had the harness made especially for Traveler. When Ben saw it, he pulled it out of the box and immediately started to examine the harness.

"Ben, when my father told me you were looking for a horse to pull your sleigh we got to work and I can't tell you how relieved I am you found one before we gave you this harness; needless to say I was sweating bullets till you pulled up with Traveler." Paul said.

Ben gave a big laugh. "Folks, I can't thank you enough, this is beautiful. Traveler is going to be so proud to wear this when he shows off pulling my sleigh. It's going to be hard to live with him. I have never seen a sleigh bell harness as nice as this, it's for sure we will not be sneaking up on any one any time soon. In fact I am going to put this on ole Traveler before I head back home tonight, thank you, thank you all, I really appreciate it." Ben humbly replied.

Paul and Angela then ask Ben if he would like to attend the Christmas Eve Church service with them later that evening. Ben graciously accepted the invitation on one condition, that he could carry everyone to church in the sleigh and the whole group would go Christmas Caroling after the service. And that is exactly what they did. It was the best Christmas Paul and his family had ever had. It combined the old traditions with some new ones that would be remembered forever by everyone in the Taylor family.

And, by the way, the jingle bell harness fit Traveler perfect.

A Life Changing Message

This particular Christmas Eve service was to be very special to Benjamin Bailey. This night, the Pastors message opened Ben's heart. Ben had heard the message of the real meaning of Christmas all of his life but tonight it finally became clear what God's ultimate gift to him was and he just needed to accept and open it. When Brother Major quoted one of his favorite quotes: "NO ONE CAN EVER BE TOO GOOD NOT TO NEED SALVATION, AND NO ONE CAN EVER BE TOO BAD TO RECEIVE SALVATION" Ben Bailey's heart was pricked and as he stepped out and made his way down the aisle to accept his Savior and seal his eternity, there was not a dry eye in the crowded little church. At the end of the aisle was Pastor Robert Major who took Ben's hand and welcomed him home on what was to be the most life changing moment of his life. From that night on, Ben attended church service practically every time the doors would open and his life was filled with a super-natural Joy and Peace that was with him for the rest of his days; but he would be very quick to tell anyone that the church attendance was not the most important thing in his Christmas miracle; not by a long shot. Benjamin Bailey's heart now belong to someone else, his name now was written in the "Lambs Book of Life."

After the service and some caroling, Ben took the Taylor family home and came in for some hot chocolate before he took his leave the night. When he was saying his goodbye for the evening, he made the statement that he was leaving to let everyone have some personal time with their own family. Ben came to Christopher standing by his sisters, who were still clutching their dollies, to say a good night. Christopher emphatically stated.

"But Mr. Ben, you are a part of our family too, you don't have to go." Arielle and Alyssa nodded their little heads in agreement with their little curls bouncing in every direction.

Ben leaned down and scooped them into his long thin arms, gathering all three at once, and gave them all a big hug. His heart was truly touched.

"You guys just gave me the best Christmas present I have ever had; God Bless all of you, and Merry Christmas." Ben said this trying to hold his emotions.

"The Lord willing I will see you all tomorrow, but before I go I was wondering if I could ask you all a very big favor this special night?" Ben inquired. Almost in unison, Paul, his father and Angela agreed, anxiously waiting to see what Ben was needing.

"Angie, I still have a few gifts to hand out tonight but I am going to need the help of JB, Paul, and I was wondering if you would let Chris come with us?" Ben asked.

Angela had noticed the bags of food and toys Ben had stored under a blanket in his sleigh when they were caroling; now she knew for sure what Ben was planning.

"Sure Santa; I mean Ben, put all of these elves to work tonight and I will have you all some more hot chocolate and coffee waiting when you return." She said with a wink.

"Great", Ben shouted. "Fellows let's get to work we don't have much time."

After a brief explanation, Ben, Paul, JB and a slightly confused Christopher hopped in the sleigh and were off to the first stop. It seems Ben had done his homework on many families in the town who had had a hard year both financially and personally. There was special gifts in every bag for all of the families. The master plan was at each house JB would hand the bags of gifts to Paul and Christopher to run to the front door, knock, then jump back into the sleigh as quick as possible before they were seen. The plan worked flawlessly and it did not take long for all to complete the job; even Traveler had become a giant reindeer on a mission as Ben would joke. After every delivery the four would all bellow out "HO HO, HO, MERRRRRY CHRISTMAS as they drove over the snow covered hills, probably renewing many a child's belief in Santa and their parent's faith the Lord would always take care of them.

After the last delivery, the four Santa's each had an ear to ear smile on their face. It was close to twenty five degrees that Christmas Eve night, but their warmed over hearts made it seem like a gentle summer's day.

On the way back Ben said. "Fellers, thanks for all of the help tonight, we make a great team, now there is going to be a few more folks that have a good Christmas."

JB and Paul broke into a verse of "JOY TO THE WORLD" in which Ben and Christopher quickly joined and sang till they reached the Taylor's home. This would be a memory of Christmas that all four men would never forget, especially Christopher. That night he had never felt so happy in his life, he had received the true

Christmas spirit, the spirit of giving. It would be with him the rest of his life.

Later, Paul and his father stepped out on the porch to bid Ben a farewell for the night and watched and listened to Traveler's new jingle bells harness fill the quiet night as Ben disappeared out of sight over the snow covered hills that cold Christmas Eve. The full moon reflected its light from the snowy landscape creating the perfect atmosphere of a soothing peace and unmatched beauty. Paul and his father just stood there both reflecting on the memories of a full day. Paul's father rested his large burly hand on his son's shoulder.

"You know Son, it's amazing how the Lord works in our lives; when Ben came back to town after his son's death I was very concerned for him. He had pretty much given up on everything, including enjoying life and was starting to get a little bitter. Then, you saw the real Benjamin Bailey and gave him a new hope with all of the kind things you and your family have done for him. Now, the real Ben Bailey that I have known all of my life is back and is happier than I have ever seen him. His decision tonight was truly a miracle. Son, I don't know when I have been as proud of you as I am today, you're a good man with a loving heart for your fellow man; you realize what really matters in life now you have helped Ben to realize it also."

Paul turned to his father and patted him on the shoulder. "Well Dad, I don't take credit for anything, I had a good teacher."

James Bennett Taylor smiled and scanned the beautiful landscape of sparkling new fallen snow one more time before retiring for the night.

"We are all so blessed. Merry Christmas, Son."

"Merry Christmas, Dad."

This would be the last Christmas Paul would share with his father.

Lit'l O's Knight

Ola Bridges was almost thirteen years old the year the war ended many years ago. She lived on a small farm with her mother, father and brother about ninety miles from Summerville. That spring the family received the tragic news her older brother had been killed in action. Upon hearing the news Ola's family went into a sadness that was almost unbearable. Her father grew silent and distant and her mother would often cry herself to sleep. Ola loved her brother and was very close to him; he gave her a nick name of Lit'l O and it stuck with her for the rest of her life. Fall was quickly approaching and on top of everything else Ola's father was worried about being able to get the crop in as he was shorthanded finding help with the harvest.

One morning just as harvest season was about to begin, Ola saw a stranger walking up the lane. He was a tall, lanky skinny fellow probably around twenty one or two years old but one could tell he had not had an easy life by just looking at him. He wore a sincere ear to ear smile and spoke in a deep southern drawl. He only carried a small knapsack. Just before he arrived at the house, Ola went and fetched her Father and Mother. The visitor was the first to speak and introduced himself. Pa Bridges was a little suspicious at first and ask.

"What can I do for you Mister?"

"Sir, I just got back from overseas a few months ago and was passing through here and was wondering if you might could give me a job for a few days?" He replied.

Pa Bridges was not much for taking in strangers but he finally agreed to let the stranger stay.

"The only thing I can offer you is a warm meal and the barn to sleep in." Pa Bridges stated.

The stranger smiled and replied.

"After the last two years I have had, those terms sound like heaven on earth to me Sir."

The two men shook hands and made it official. For the next few weeks the stranger was up before sunrise and did every job he could for the Bridges family from repairing the barn and the house to bringing in the crops. Soon he was invited to spend the evenings with the family and would bring some long overdue laughter back into the house. He had a book of stories with him of just about anything you could think of. One of the stories was about the medieval Knights in shining armor, this was Lit'l O's favorite. She loved the part when the Knight would save someone's life and make everything right. It wasn't long until Lit'l O started confiding in the stranger about losing her big brother and how sad her father and mother had been. She told him a story of how her brother loved the aroma of her father's pipe and how he had not smoked it since he heard the sad news, how her mother use to love to sing around the house as she would cook and sew, and how they all would pray together at the end of the day, and talk, and laugh. The stranger could see that grief was destroying this family.

When harvest was over, it had come time for the stranger to leave the Bridges. The night before he left he thanked them for taking him in for a while. The next morning he said his goodbye to the family. Lit'l O knew he had to leave but she was heartbroken, when it came time for him to say goodbye both had tears in their eyes. The stranger took something out of his pocket and gave it to Lit'l O. It was a small brown bag. He told her in a low voice to give this to her Pa and Ma but only after he was long gone. She honored his request and gave the brown bag to her father and mother that night. Pa Bridges opened the bag and inside was a tobacco pouch full of his favorite tobacco, also a crude slightly dirty envelope with a letter and the book of stories he read to them. When he opened the envelope the letter was holding money, which fell out on the table. Pa Bridges read the letter out loud. It told how the stranger had gone to war on the same train as their son and the pleasant conversation they struck up. He had expressed his love for his parents and his little sister and how much he was worried about not being there to helped them. The letter continued to ask the family to remember their son as a hero and honor him every day by living their lives and being happy and thankful. The letter finished by expressing how it was an honor to meet them and how much he appreciated their kindness. The book of stories was for Lit'l O and signed on the inside cover. It read.

"Someday you will find your Knight." It was signed Benjamin Bailey.

Something happened to the Bridges family that night, it was a new joy the stranger had help bring. Prayer would return to the family. Pa Bridges said he had never met a better man, Ma Bridges thought he could have been an angel, but to Lit'l O; he was her Knight in shining armor that she would never forget.

227

That evening Ben Bailey met JB Taylor at the train station to return to Summerville. JB Taylor had also visited another family that had lost their son. On the way home the two men talked about the families they had met and the eleven more they were planning to see on their personal mission. The conversation slowed to silence after a while when Ben said sadly.

"You know JB, every time I ride the No 2, I can't help thinking about those guys who never came back and it tears me up inside. Here we are the only two that came back alive."

James Taylor took a deep breath before answering. "I know my friend, but the way I see it is; you and I will never let them be forgotten, maybe we made it back just for that reason, to help the families that lost their sons."

"You're right JB; you're right." Ben replied after a few moments in thought.

The two friends then slumped down in their seats and closed their weary eyes for the long trip home on the Ole No 2.

About ten years would go by and Lit'l O had grown into a beautiful woman. She left the farm to get an education. She took jobs and saved her money the best she could to secure a career. She had discovered she was very handy with math and was offered a position in Summerville in bookkeeping at the court house. One day she was walking home and she noticed a man loading his truck with supplies. As she got closer, she could not believe her eyes. She approached the man and ask.

"Are you Mr. Bailey, are you Mr. Benjamin Bailey?" She ask desperately.

The man turned around and replied.

"Yes Ma'am, I am, but most people just call me Ben."

Lit'l O nervously reached into her handbag and pulled out the book he gave her years ago and with tears streaming down her cheeks.

"Maybe they do call you Ben, but I call you my Knight in Shining Armor." She cried.

Ben could hardly believe his eyes, he had barely recognized her. She was the most beautiful women he had ever seen.

"What happened to all of those freckles?" He asked jokingly.

"They finally fell off, I guess they got tired of me trying to rub them off so they just gave up." She replied laughing and crying at the same time.

"Well Lit'l O, you might have lost those freckles but haven't lost your sense of humor; do you have time for a cold drink and catching up time?" Ben joyfully suggested.

"Oh yes, yes, that would be wonderful." She replied.

This was the start of a new life for both Ben and Lit'l O together. After about a year the twenty nine year old Ben realized she was the love of his life. They were married in the old Bailey mansion with Ben's best man being JB Taylor. Every day Ben realized just how much he loved her and she returned his love. After a few years they had a son. Lit'l O only lived a few days after their son was born. Not only Ben, but the whole town was saddened. Until this, Ben Bailey never knew how much the townsfolk loved him and Lit'l O. She had asked to be buried on the little farm where they had met. Ben tried very hard, but he could not escape the grief and the reminders of their life together, there were so many happy memories and personal touches in the old Bailey home now that Lit'l O had provided, the old place had come alive with joy; now, she was gone. Ben could hardly bare living there anymore. He finally decided to leave his home town thinking he would never return. He moved near the farm where he first met her. Lit'l O's parents were still there and were happy they could see their only grandson grow up. Ben would help them on their farm as long as they lived and Ma and Pa Bridges helped take care of their grandson. They would visit Litl'O's grave often and Ben would tell his son all about his mother. The only other person he confided in now was his best friend James Bennett Taylor who would come to see him whenever he could.

When Ben's son reached manhood he entered the Marine Corps. Another war had broken out and he was severely wounded while carrying one of his buddies to safety. He was sent home and Ben would take care of him until the aftermath of his wounds took his life. Ben laid his son to rest next to his mother that he never knew. Christopher Bennett Bailey would receive the Congressional Medal of Honor for his heroic deed. Ben kept it with him wherever he went.

Many years later after he lost his only son, Benjamin Bailey would come to realize the people of his little home town were still his friends, just older like himself, but now, he was all alone in this world. After many heart to heart talks with his best friend; Benjamin Bailey decided to quietly move back to Summerville; a much older and broken man who had started privately questioning his faith.

Winter Excitement

It was the first part of the New Year now and winter had set in to the town to stay for a few months. The ground would stay frozen as hard as a rock making it impossible to treasure hunt till the spring thaw. This was especially frustrating to Christopher as one of his Christmas gifts was a state of the art Metal Detector. Paul and Angela decided Christopher was old enough now to have his own detector and were very proud of their son and how he had matured enough to be responsible and take care of it and follow the "Treasure hunters creed."Paul was even more proud his son had kept the stolen gold secret through everything that had happened to him over the last few months. He understood his frustration at not being able to use his new machine. The bright side was Christopher could read up on how to use it properly and take care of it. Christopher strategically placed it on top of his dresser so he could see it every night before he went to sleep; but this waiting for the earth to thaw out was total torture for him.

Paul was still doing research on the stage robbery and had asked Ben when it was a good time to meet as he wanted to tell him the whole story. Oddly enough, Ben had something he needed to talk to Paul about also. He seemed very anxious to get together with both Paul and Christopher. They agreed on an evening that week to meet and talk at Paul's house. Angela invited Ben for dinner and afterward Paul, Ben and Christopher went into the drawing room to talk. The three got comfortable on the couch and leather chair strategically situated by the big crackling roaring fire.

"Now fellers, what is it you have on your minds?" Ben inquired, while absorbing the heat of the flames.

"Well Ben, maybe you'd better not get too comfortable because I have a long story to tell you that will require a lot of show and tell." Paul answered.

Ben leaned forward in the old leather chair getting more curious by the minute.

"This is beginning to sound a bit serious Paul." Ben said.

"It could be, but I think if you like a mystery story, you are going to love what Christopher and I have discovered." Paul continued.

"This is getting more exciting by the minute, I'm ready to hear the story when you are ready to tell it, and I'm all ears." Ben laughed.

"Ben, I think it would be better just to start off by showing you some documents I found. Follow me; I've got something very interesting to show you upstairs." Paul answered.

Paul led Ben and Christopher upstairs talking about his discovery all the way. As they climbed the stairs,

Paul told Christopher that he was going to let him in on another secret, a secret room.

"We have a secret room wow, that's neat, where is it Dad?" Christopher quizzed.

"I'm getting ready to show you and Ben: but Christopher, this has to remain secret, no one else can know about it, I just thought you are big enough now and trustworthy to know where I got the old newspapers." Paul answered.

Ben was starting to look bewildered while becoming more intrigued. The three reached the octagon room at the end of the hall and Paul showed Ben and Christopher the secret room and explained the whole story of the stagecoach robbery to Ben. Ben was fairly silent except for a few short questions while Paul explained. Paul could tell the wheels in his brain were turning, as he had the same look on his face as when he would tell one of his stories. Usually he would get a slight smile with a mischievous look on his face. "So you think it is a good chance the stolen gold could still be out there and even somewhere on my property." Ben asked.

"For the sake of having a great adventure, and solving a long forgotten mystery, yes Ben, I think the gold is still hidden, and I think it's hidden somewhere on your land; all of our research points that way." Paul exclaimed.

"Well fellers, this is all very interesting so I think I should warn you to get ready for the beginning of an even greater adventure, cause while I was making repairs on my old sleigh; I found this little lady in my barn." Ben exclaimed.

Ben pulled back his coat and put his thumb and forefinger in his vest watch pocket; then with an effortless action flipped out a shiny 1876 twenty dollar gold coin which landed with a heavy thump and a slow spinning action on the small antique table.

Is That What I Think It Is?

$\mathcal{A}$s the spinning coin came to a rest, Paul and Christopher stood in front of the little table speechless. Neither had ever seen a twenty dollar gold coin in the flesh and it was one of Paul's dreams to someday dig one up. When Ben saw their reaction he just chuckled. "You two look like you've seen a ghost; this is the reason I needed to talk to you boys to show you what I had found in the barn. I'm glad now you told me your story before I told you mine; it made the night a whole lot more interesting." He mused.

Paul reached to pick up the coin and examined it with nervous excitement. It was one of the most beautiful coins he had ever seen. At this time he wasn't even thinking about how this could be one of the stolen coins from the stagecoach robbery. He must have turned it over and over to examine it a hundred times in his shaking hands before he passed it to an equal excited Christopher to examine. Then it hit him like a ton of bricks, could this possibly be one of the stolen coins perhaps hidden somewhere in Ben's barn or just a random coin some poor soul lost over a hundred years ago? After all the old news article did say Samuel Bailey was captured in the Bailey barn.

Paul turned to Ben and started pelting him with every question he could think of concerning the details of his discovery. Ben calmly sat down in one of the old rocking chairs in the tower; made himself comfortable and began to tell his story of the discovery as only he could.

"Well, let's see fellers, let me just start from the beginning. After I finished the renovations and repairs on the old sleigh, I was looking for a better place to store it in the barn. I found the perfect area as I could hook up

Traveler to the sleigh and we could be out and about in record time with minimum problems. Funny thing about that ole boy, many a morning after a big snow I'll find him already backed into the position to be hooked up for a sleigh ride; but that's another story."

Ben would often go off track when he was telling a story, but Paul realized that was part of his art of storytelling.

"Anyway, about a week ago I was cleaning the area for storage and while pulling back some loose hay I saw this little lady shining just begging to be picked up. Why, she was not even buried, just lying there under the hay, no telling how long it's been there or who lost it, although I have a feeling we have a good chance of finding out after listening to your story Paul. Sounds to me like Sam Bailey may have been a little bit careless with this little beauty. It also looks like I may have a scalawag as one of my ancestors." Ben finished.

Paul admitted to Ben he was dreading to tell him the part of the story that Samuel Bailey was the real robber and not the alias name he was using. But all in all Ben took the news well; his take on it was, it was in the past and there was nothing he could do about it. Ben then recalled that he possessed an old Bailey family Bible, full of records and genealogy. Paul volunteered to help him go through it hoping maybe they could find out more information on the real Samuel Bailey. But after learning one of his ancestors stole money from the hard working farmers and ranchers of long ago Summerville, Ben wasn't so sure he wanted to know more about what he now considered a black sheep of the family.

Ben rubbed his chin a few times, which usually meant he was hatching a plan.

"Fellers, I just had a thought. Since Chris here has a brand new treasure hunting machine, and the ground in my barn is not frozen like the rest of the earth now, what do you think about you fellers coming over and searching the barn; you might find a few more of these golden ladies?"

Christopher immediately answered. "Dad that sounds neat, do you think we can go Saturday, I can try out my detector?"

Paul tried to hide his own excitement of the idea and paused a minute to check his mental schedule.

"Christopher, I see no reason to turn down that invitation whatsoever." Paul exclaimed.

"Well then; it's agreed." Ben interjected. "Saturday we officially start our hidden gold hunting adventure and it will be our little secret or in this case, our big secret."Needless to say Paul and Christopher did not get much sleep for the next few days hoping they were one step closer to finding the hidden stagecoach gold that disappeared so long ago.

Searching The Barn

It seemed like Saturday would never come but it finally arrived and Paul and Christopher showed up at Ben's farm bright and early. It was a very cold and crisp day and a new snow had fallen the night before, but at least the three would be hunting inside the barn where it would be a tad warmer. Ben had risen early and cooked them a big breakfast with all of the trimmings. Paul was ashamed of himself for gobbling it down so quickly in order to start the treasure hunt even earlier. During the meal, Ben talked about his old family Bible he had uncovered in one of the bedrooms. He had already started a curious search for any information on Samuel Bailey. Paul could only speculate on what Ben's thoughts were about one of his ancestors being a thief and he was anxious to see if Ben would uncover any information on this mystery.

Ben had brought the Bible down and put in on the old kitchen table. The leather bound book was over a hundred and fifty years old and had much of the Bailey family history and family tree recorded in the front and rear sections. Ben explained to Christopher that even before the birth of America this was the only way to preserve the history of your family. The Bible was in remarkably good shape for its age and Paul resisted the temptation to start probing into it until they had finished the treasure hunt for the day.

During breakfast Christopher was filling in Ben on his new metal detector he received for Christmas. Ben had plenty of questions on how it operated and it gave Christopher a grown up feeling to explain its operation and answer Ben's questions before the big barn hunt. Paul enjoyed observing Ben becoming one of Christopher's trusted friends.

After breakfast the three eager treasure hunters made their way to the huge two story barn that had weathered the elements for over one hundred and fifty years. When they opened the door, Traveler gave them a good morning grunt while Ben fixed him a breakfast of oats and fresh water. Paul helped Christopher in setting his detector since this was the first time he had tried it out on a real treasure hunt. Paul had decided not to bring his detector this time. If there were any lost coins in Ben's barn; he wanted Christopher to find them. He knew it would be one of those special memories his son would carry for the rest of his life. This was Paul and Ben's little secret plan just between them. The barn's dirt floor surface area was very large and was going to be hard to navigate even for a professional coin shooter so Paul laid out the hunting area by marking them in huge squares with old strips of lumber. Christopher would scan each square by crisscrossing them thoroughly before proceeding to the next section. Paul did not want to miss covering one square inch of ground. The team started where Ben had uncovered the gold coin and would hunt the whole area by the end of the frigid day. To their disappointment, the only thing they found was a few old square nails and a 1936 Buffalo nickel. At least the nickel helped to alleviate Christopher's disappointment a little but Ben could tell Paul was still disheartened. Paul chalked it up as good experience for Christopher; in order to get familiar with his new detector and those days of disappointment.It was getting late and all three men were becoming tired so they decided to call it a day and go home to start thinking about the big treasure hunt when the earth was thawed out. It could not come soon enough for any of them.The next step was to go through Ben's family Bible with a fine tooth comb to search for clues. Maybe they would find something, anything that could clue them in on where to start the next search. They were all more determined than ever to either find the stolen gold coins or find out what could have become of them. Paul did not express his thoughts out loud as he did not think Ben's family Bible would yield much information on the stolen treasure. Little did he realize the old family Bible was about to launch one of the greatest adventures of his lifetime.

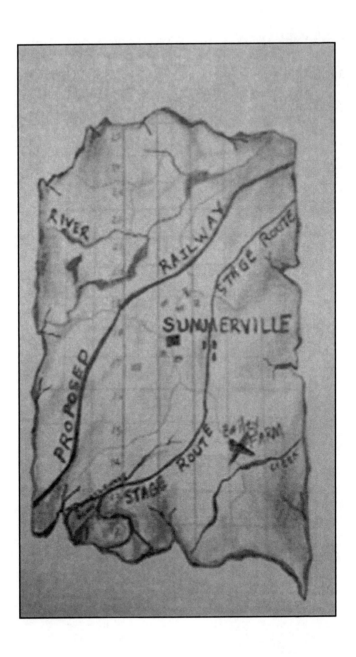

The Family Bible

Just a few days later Paul met with Ben at his house to start to search the Bailey family Bible hoping to find information and any clue that might point them in the right direction. Christopher had returned to school now from the Christmas and New Year's vacation and was unable to be there and Paul didn't know if he was more upset about going back to school or not being able to go with him to Ben's house. He surmised it was a little of both as he remembered how hard it was for him to return to school after any type of vacation when he was Christopher's age.

Ben made a pot of coffee and he and Paul sat down at the kitchen table and proceeded to examine the historical Bible. The book was larger than any Bible Paul had ever seen. Paul could only imagine the experiences and travels this book had witnessed. It had traveled with the Bailey family and had made it to Summerville, its final home, in a covered wagon. It was well constructed with a leather cover that folded over the end of the pages to protect them. Even without the extra letters and documents that had been stored between some of the pages; it was still about five inches thick. It had a large brass snap latch located about three inches from the end of the cover where a strap from the back cover could wrap around and snap into the latch, which needed a key to open. Ben's late mother gave the only key that existed to him just a few days before she passed away. As Paul examined the outside of the Bible he asked Ben.

"How long has it been since you opened this Bible, Ben?" Ben paused, took a deep breath and exhaled it in a sad manner.

"Well Paul, I'm really ashamed to tell you, but I haven't opened this book since my mother died almost fifty years ago."

For the first time Paul now saw a serious and more solemn side of his new friend. Ben started explaining.

"My mother was one of the greatest women I ever knew and I was fairly young when she passed. It's hard to explain, but for a while I didn't have the will or maybe the interest in looking through the family Bible and I stayed away from family history and became slightly bitter; I guess I just put it away and never got around to opening it. Nobody has opened it since." Ben finished. Paul paused for a moment, before he responded. He had the greatest respect for Ben and did not want to tread on his feelings or personal life. At that moment he realized there are many more important things in life than chasing down lost gold coins. Paul stopped and leaned back in the old kitchen chair. Ben immediately noticed the sudden change in Paul and inquired if he was alright. He made light of it by asking Paul if his coffee tasted that bad. Paul laughed and explained his concerns to Ben. Ben folded his arms and leaned back in his chair, then answered.

"Paul, I appreciate your feelings and you don't need to be concerned. If I had a problem with opening up the past I wouldn't have suggested searching this grand old book of family history. I think it will probably be a little bittersweet realizing my mother was the last person to enter any history or information in it; but when you think about it, it's kind of exciting. Do you remember when you told me one of the best things you enjoyed when you were treasure hunting, was not so much finding the treasure itself, but trying to imagine the last person that actually touched it, or who it belonged to; especially after being buried or lost for over a hundred years? That was the real reason you liked discovering it so much; not so much the discovery, but the history behind it. Well, I understand what you mean now, because I feel the same way about going through the old family Bible. Tell you what, let's just consider it a treasure hunt without having to dig in the dirt." Ben exclaimed. Paul paused and nodded his head in agreement.

"Thanks Ben, that makes me feel one hundred per cent better about this." Paul answered.

"Good. Now that that's settled, let's see what kind of skeletons we can rattle." Ben said reverting to his old self while chuckling.

Ben inserted the key in the brass latch, made a small turn to the right releasing the lock with a snap. This was going to be a painstaking task but now both men were looking forward to revisiting some Bailey family history as well as searching for buried treasure clues. After he pulled the key out of the latch he told Paul. "I'm going to let you take it from here, son; you are more of an expert on how to handle old papers and documents, I will just try to answer any questions for you that might come up." Ben explained.

"Well, OK." Paul answered.

Paul gently opened the old Bible revealing the Bailey genealogy at the front with a few unsealed letters in between some of the pages.

"The first thing I am curious about is what is mentioned about Sam Bailey." Paul said. Usually family Bibles would tell something about the person's origin and other interesting facts other than just their birth and death; a legacy of their accomplishments. Paul slowly skimmed down the family tree and there it was; Samuel Andrew Bailey, Born 1853, Died 1876. Paul could not find any more history of details on Sam Bailey other than this. Usually there would be something more. The strange thing was that every other Bailey ancestor had some kind of history and other details connected to their name. Samuel Bailey had nothing. Paul pointed this out to Ben asking him why he thought Sam was entered in that way. Ben answered.

"Well Paul, this is just my opinion but I believe it could be one of two reasons. One is he didn't accomplish much in his life as he was only about twenty three years old when he died; and the other is the family just entered him in the Bible as a courtesy only, because they were ashamed of him."

Paul nodded his head in agreement. "Maybe we will find some more information about him as we search." Paul exclaimed.

Paul worked out an agreement with Ben that any letters or other sealed documents he uncovered, he would give to Ben to read while he went over the rest of the recorded information with a little more attention. After about two hours of searching and two pots of coffee, Ben discovered an old map that looked like the railroad company had printed. It had a makeshift map of the little town of Summerville on it and the proposed route the train would follow.

"Maybe we need to study this a little closer." Ben cried. Paul leaned over to get a closer look. "I think your right Ben, look, this map not only has the proposed future railroad coming through town but it also has the old stagecoach route marked." Paul exclaimed

Paul scanned the map from left to right very carefully not to miss any details.

"Ben, look at this, I don't believe it." Paul announced excitedly.

"What's that, Paul?" Ben questioned.

"Not only does this have the old stagecoach route carefully marked it also has your patch of land marked as the "Bailey Farm "with the location of your house and a scale of miles so you can figure the distance." Ben, you have discovered a document that can help us pinpoint where the stage was robbed. This is great, absolutely great." Paul exclaimed.

"Well just glad I could be of service Son." Ben said with a hearty laugh.

Paul and Ben spent another two hours searching the Bible but did not find anything more significant that would have anything to do with the gold search. Both men agreed in their conversation that it was going to be a long winter just trying to plan the treasure hunt before spring thaw.

For the rest of the winter, Paul revisited the old newspaper articles on the stage robbery to make sure he did not overlook any helpful information. Ben and Christopher also did their part digging up any family history that might give some desperately needed clues to the location of the treasure. This was one mission all three enjoyed, however; it still did not make the long cold winter any shorter.

Spring Fever Or Gold Fever

Spring was finally showing signs of taking over Summerville, cleansing the earth as it made the long cold winter another chapter in history. New sprigs of green grass were piercing their way through the newly thawed earth; the streams and lakes were filing to the brim with fresh crystal clear water from the melted snow. Cattlemen were busy tending to the new calves and colts being born to the herds; farmers were speculating which crops would yield more revenue and how many acres to plant in the coming season. Everything was just about as it normally was at springtime in the valley. Paul and Ben had spent most of their free time following up on the old railroad maps and newspaper articles.

One evening Paul was once again reading the articles in the old newspapers and came across something he had missed. The article said the stage was robbed near "Rattlesnake Bend." Paul had read this article probably a hundred times and only at this reading did Rattlesnake Bend catch his attention. Paul retrieved the old map and carefully opened the yellowed document slowly scanning it for anything new. There were many labels of locations on the map in very tiny print. Paul pulled out a magnifying glass from the drawer and proceeded to look closer to the fine print on the old stagecoach road. As he slowly scanned the road starting from the town to the rural outskirts he came across the location named "Rattlesnake Bend" which was all but hidden in one of the worn folds of the map. Paul shouted out a big YEAH, this was another big break he had been hoping to find. Now, all they had to do was locate Rattlesnake Bend and start detecting from that point. As soon as he could, Paul showed Christopher and Ben what he had found.

"Ben, in all of your early days of living here have you ever heard of anyone mentioning a place on the old road called Rattlesnake Bend?" Paul asked.

"Not that I can recall. Do you think it has been renamed something else or maybe just forgotten about?" Ben asked.

Then Paul had a thought. Maybe his Aunt Evelyn could remember or even know someone in town that knew where it was located. If they could find this spot, this is definitely where the treasure hunt would begin. Paul's plan was to back track the area back to Ben's farm in as wide of a sweep as possible, looking for landmarks Samuel Bailey might have used to mark the place where he could have buried the illusive gold.

Rattlesnake Bend

*P*aul wasted no time in contacting Aunt Evelyn. He stopped by her house after running a small errand for Angela. Aunt Evelyn was glad to see Paul as both of them had been busy that spring just preparing for the challenges it would always bring after a hard winter, and visiting time had been scarce. Paul caught his Aunt repotting flowers she had planted in the winter. She always had the most beautiful flower garden in the county and was especially known for her rare orchids she grew. Every year she would supply Paul and his high school friends with a beautiful corsage for the prom. Her secret was planting early but only if you were sure Jack Frost was out of commission for the season. Paul grabbed a pot or two and pitched in while explaining what he had uncovered while updating his Aunt on his missing gold investigation. When asked about Rattlesnake Bend, Aunt Evelyn stopped her chore and slowly went into a serious thought. "You know, I haven't heard anyone mention Rattlesnake Bend in a long time, in fact, I was still a small girl the last time I heard that term, but I know exactly where it is; and it certainly did live up to its name because any vehicle had to almost crawl at a snail's pace to get through it without having an accident; in fact, that is one of the main reasons the new road was cut through to town bypassing the bend. I can still remember as a little girl passing through there, it was always scary."

"Where exactly is it located?" Paul asked.

Aunt Evelyn started to explain the location then stopped in mid-sentence. "Well Paul, what if I just show you; it's a beautiful spring day and I need some fresh air, let's just take a break and hop in your truck and go see it, it's not far from here but we might have to do some walking."

"Sounds great, I'm ready when you are." Paul exclaimed.

Making good conversation as they traveled, the two reached the location of Rattlesnake Bend in fairly good time. It was just outside of town and now far from the beaten path but the road had not been used in many years. Paul now understood how it got its name. Although the rocks on either side of the small path would not be considered mountains, they were too steep to bypass with any type of vehicle much less a stage coach and they curved in an S shape for about three hundred yards. As he and Aunt Evelyn surveyed the area Paul was thinking how Sam Bailey had picked the perfect spot for a hold up. At one point the road appeared to dead end into a huge boulder then made a sharp turn to the left. Nothing on wheels could make it through the bend with any speed. As you came to the end of the crooked road, one could still make out the grass covered sunken wheel ruts that were still visible from so long ago. Yes, Sam Bailey had definitely done his homework in planning his heist of the gold at this forsaken place. Paul could see now it was going to be even more time consuming hunting for the treasure but this was definitely going to be the starting point.

As Paul and Aunt Evelyn walked back to the truck, Aunt Evelyn stopped and turned around for one last look at Rattlesnake Bend before they left."You know. Paul, it's hard to believe as a little girl we traveled on this old road. I remember one day our family was coming back from Oakville from visiting relatives; it was getting late and I remember being scared to death of this stretch of the road as Papa would carefully navigate through it. Now it's just a memory, although still a very clear memory; the years have certainly passed by so quickly. That seemed like it happened just last week." She commented almost under her breath. For a few moments, Aunt Evelyn was silent and seemed to be reliving pieces of her childhood of simpler but harder days. She looked over at Paul and smiled all the while knowing he understood her and how she liked an adventure but now she was starting to realize she was becoming a bit slower. Paul smiled back at her and broke the silence.

"Well Aunt Evelyn, we are getting ready to start looking for the lost gold soon, do you want to join us for our great treasure hunt?" Paul asked.

"You just never know, I would love to be there when you find it, but I think I'll play it by ear so don't wait on me." She answered. "Fair enough, I sure appreciate you showing me my starting point." Paul replied.

Aunt Evelyn smiled."It was just nice to spend some time with you again, Paul."

Paul and Aunt Evelyn climbed back into the truck.

"You know the best thing about going home now?" Paul jested.

"What's that Paul?" Aunt Evelyn inquired.

"We don't have to drive through Rattlesnake Bend to get there."

"Good point son." Aunt Evelyn replied along with her special laugh.

The Great Treasure Hunt

Spring was now in full swing in Summerville and Paul, Ben and Christopher had done everything they knew to do to prepare for the gold hunt. They would start early next Saturday morning at Rattlesnake Bend with the plan to backtrack as close to the old stage coach road as possible eventually ending up back at Ben's barn. They all were aware of the possible long and disappointing days ahead but all had agreed to make a fun adventure out of it even if they came up empty handed. Both Paul and Christopher were going to use their own detectors to cover more ground. The earth was in perfect condition to treasure shoot as it was not too wet and not too dry and hard. The next

Saturday the three met at Rattlesnake Bend to officially begin the hunt. Paul mapped out sections of ground where it was possible to sweep as not to overlook a square inch of ground. Paul used baking flour to mark the spots in hopes it would not rain at night to wash it away. Much of the terrain was rocky making it easier to scan while not permitting much digging. This could make it faster to cover the area.

Paul knew this hunt would test Christopher as to whether he would stick it out to the end or get discouraged and lose interest. He was hoping they would find something even if it had nothing to do with the gold just to keep up their momentum. Since it was spring and the Rattlers were feeling extra aggressive, Ben decided to help watch out for trouble. And, of course, he brought his trusty ax along just for insurance.

It was about midday now and the pair had not found anything; not even a tiniest of tones had Paul or Christopher received on the detectors. They took a break for lunch and by now had hunted about half way through the pass when Christopher's detector made a slight beep. He could not tell what the object was by the tone or by his indicator needle, but it sounded like a solid piece of metal. After a few passes, he pinpointed the object and marked it with a small rock then called his father over to investigate. Paul hurried to the sight and started to carefully dig around the object and had Christopher wave his detector over the area as he separated the dirt. Paul finally felt the object with his digging tool then carefully pulled it along with a clump of dirt out of the shallow hole. He then wiped off all of the caked on dirt and tried to identify Christopher's find. It looked like some kind of large shell casing. It had turned a turquoise green and appeared to be made of brass and was in good shape considering.

"What is it Dad?" Christopher asked.

"Well, I'm not sure." Paul answered.

By then Ben had come over to check it out."Is this a rifle or pistol shell casing Ben?" Paul questioned.

Ben took a closer look."I haven't seen one of these in years, I think this is an old, and I do mean old, shotgun shell casing. This is the way they manufactured them over a hundred years ago; they were made out of brass." Ben explained.

They took the shell back to the truck and cleaned it with some water. The shell had inscription on the flat head side that read, "ST LOUIS SHELL CO 10GA. Paul recalled the newspaper article that described the stage driver wounding Samuel Bailey in the leg, but the article did not specify how many shots the driver fired.

"Let's go back to the site and see if we can find any more of these shell casings. We will both hunt it thoroughly and call it a day; if this is what I think it is we may be on to something." Paul exclaimed.

"What are you thinking?" Ben asked.

Paul held up the shotgun shell casing between his fingers while turning and inspecting it over and over again. "Ben, this could be the shotgun shell that wounded

Samuel Bailey when he robbed the stage that day; a wound that ultimately killed him." He answered.

Christopher's eyes widened. "Wow Dad, do you really think that is what it is?"

"We'll take it home and do some investigating on this little gem; you may have just found another key clue; good job Son." Paul answered.

"That goes for me to Chris; you are a natural at this treasure hunting business." Ben added.

Paul and Ben could almost see Christopher's proud chest swelling as he examined the shell casing. They looked at each other and smiled.

Paul took the shell casing home and checked it out in one of his reference books on the history of firearms and ammunition. It seems a company manufactured this particular shell by the name of Conical Shell Company. The information that was so intriguing to Paul was the dates it was manufactured; only from 1874 to 1881. The article also alluded to the fact that this ammunition was widely used in the old short double barrel shotguns used on the stagecoach lines for security. Paul was hoping this was the shotgun casing that carried the buckshot that wounded Samuel Bailey and not just a discarded shell used by a random hunter so long ago.

More Hunting

The days were becoming longer now as spring became middle aged and the treasure hunters had made much progress as far as covering ground, however, no progress was being made in the gold finding department. Ben's house was now in viewing distance as the crew slowly but thoroughly hunted the old stage road. Sometimes it was difficult to follow as the weather and time had steadily worked together over the long years to erase all trace of the path that was once a well-traveled road. One Positive note was Paul and Christopher and even Ben were finding a few arrowheads on top of the ground; especially after a brief spring rain that would wash away the loose dirt and reveal the ancient flints exposed by mother earth. Christopher had quite a collection of arrowheads that he and his father had randomly discovered while metal detecting. The flawless ones had been beautifully framed and were hanging on Christopher's bedroom wall.

Early Saturday morning on the second weekend in April, the crew was out once again strategically searching the ground not to miss an inch of area, when Paul received a deep tone on the Gold Duster. He was hunting in a small hilly area with the dirt mounds rising up just a few inches from the level road area. Ben said he thought it might be an abandoned home of a family of Ground Hogs. Nevertheless the dirt was thin, almost sandy to the touch. As Paul was sweeping the detector slowly over the area he received a deep short tone. He cleared the machine and swiped over the area again and again each time picking up a deep unusual tone. On the last pass over on the area he checked the meter. The needle was frozen on the gold reading. Paul's heart began to pump just a little faster.

He called to Christopher to go to the truck and bring him the sifter he had custom made himself. The sifter had a wire bottom with the wire just wide enough to let the dirt pass through revealing even the smallest of objects caught in the basket; perfect for the type of soil they were hunting on. By now Ben had come over to check out the situation just as Christopher arrived with the sifter. Paul was still passing the Gold Duster over the area multiple times attempting to pinpoint the object as close as possible.

"Boys, my machine is registering gold in this hole." Paul announced excitingly.

Paul then turned to Christopher."Son, do you want to dig this one?" He asked. Christopher got an excited look on his face, and then suddenly paused before he answered.

"No Dad, I think you should do it." He answered.

"Are you sure son?" Paul questioned again.

"Yes Dad, I'm sure, I think you should dig this one." He said grinning.

Ben then interjected. "Tell you what, why don't you two both work on it and I will hold this flour sifter contraption and we can see what is down there."

"Sounds like a good plan men; we will do it together." Paul said. All three were getting excited and preceded to work on the dig. Paul marked the area with his digger and started to carefully pull out dirt from the area and place it in different piles stopping only to sweep the detector over the piles each time to see if the object had been pulled from the hole. The object was fairly deep and as they got closer the tone became even deeper while the needle held steady on the "GOLD "setting.

"Let's hope the Gold Duster is telling us the truth on this one." Paul exclaimed.

After the fourth pile of dirt had been lifted out of the hole, Paul waved the detector head across the open pit one more time. This time there was no tone.

"OK fellas, I think we may have pulled the mystery item out of the hole." Paul said. Let's start searching these piles one by one." Paul exclaimed.

Paul hovered the wand over the first pile of dirt. No tone. Then, he scanned the second pile. Again, there was no tone. On the third pile, Paul received a beautiful deep tone unlike any he had ever experienced. Ben held the sifter while Paul and Christopher carefully transferred the dirt into it.

"Now Ben, slowly shake the sifter away from the other piles." Paul instructed. Ben picked a bare spot and began to shake the sifter from side to side while the other two watched intently. As the dirt passed through the wire mesh at the bottom of the sifter the three started to hear a slight rattling sound as the dirt disappeared to reveal the object that had been so patiently courted. Finally, there it was. A beautiful gold coin."-Jumping Jehoshaphat fellers; it's another gold coin." Ben shouted.

All three hunters just took a moment and stared at the coin in frozen amazement.

"This is unbelievable." Paul exclaimed.

"Wow Dad, you finally found a gold coin." Christopher shouted.

"Well, who's going to touch it first?" Ben asked.

"I think Dad should." Christopher interjected.

"I agree with Chris, Paul, you've been waiting for this day to come since you were knee high to a grasshopper. This is your day, Son." Ben said with a big grin on his face.

Speechless, Paul reached into the sifter and picked up the coin. It was another1876 twenty dollar gold piece, which looked brand new. Paul passed it around to Ben and Christopher to study. They took it to the truck and washed the remaining stubborn dirt off with water. The coin was absolutely flawless.

"Guys, this has to be another one of those stolen coins; there is just no other explanation for it to be at this location. I think Sam Bailey dropped this coin on his way to Ben's barn so long ago." Paul said.

While looking at the coin over and over again. Ben added. "I think your right Paul, I have a really good feeling the rest of his loot is hidden somewhere between here and my farm if not somewhere even closer." Ben exclaimed.

The sun was quickly going down and after the excited hunters promised each other to keep the fantastic find a secret, they said their goodbyes for the night. Each realizing they were not going to get much sleep after their exciting discovery of the day. On the way home, Paul was curious about Christopher's actions at the discovery of the coin.

"Son, I am curious about something. Why did you not want to dig for the coin today?"

Christopher was still closely examining the coin turning it over and over again in his little dirty hands. Without hesitation he answered his father.

"Well Dad, I knew that you had said you always wanted to find a gold coin one day, so I thought it would make you happy if that's what it was and you could dig it up."

Paul got a lump in his throat he almost couldn't hide from his son while pausing a moment before replying. "Son, you are really something, I really appreciate that act of kindness. I am so proud of you."

"I'm proud of you too Dad." He answered still examining the coin intently as they drove home. The rest of the drive home, Paul realized the coin wasn't the only gold in that homeward bound truck. He realized Christopher had a heart of gold that far outweighed anything he could ever discover in a lifetime by putting others needs and joys before his own. His son was starting to grow up. It had been another good day.

Impatience

Another spring rain had set in for a few days making it impossible to hunt and adding to the impatience of Paul and Christopher's mission. The great thing was it had stopped on Friday and it would be possible to continue the hunt all day Saturday. The hunter's excitement far out weighed having to deal with the muddy terrain. During the week all Paul and Christopher could talk about at home was their discovery with Angela and Arielle and Alyssa, who were too young to realize the importance but still liked to look at the coin with their brother. Paul and Angela would laugh to themselves when they heard Christopher telling his sisters of his adventures and showing them his metal detector. Paul let Christopher keep the coin in his room with strict instructions of the importance of keeping the find top secret, something he had become very good at.When Saturday came Paul and Christopher went by and picked Ben up early. Ben was extra cheery that morning."You know Paul, I've been thinking, now see if you agree. I am not an expert like you guys at this treasure hunting game, but it seems to me we have something going for us in this hunt that gives us a great advantage."

"What's that Mr. Ben?" Christopher asked."Well, for as long as I can remember, this land has not changed one bit except maybe some of the old trees are gone now, but the rocks haven't moved so maybe we can try to think like that scalawag ancestor of mine and find a place that he marked in order to return and retrieve his loot." Ben replied.

Paul thought for a moment."That's real good thinking Ben; you may turn into a master treasure hunter your-self one day." Paul said. They both laughed as Paul continued."But actually when you think about it, you're right. If the gold is still hidden, my theory is Sam Bailey did not know he would be caught and might have been trying to lighten his load. He had not planned on getting wounded in the leg. If that was the case he would have buried the heavy bags of gold in an easy to find place he would recognize when he returned for it. We will have to search every inch of land very carefully, especially now that we have discovered a loose coin." Paul added. The hunters picked up at the place of the great discovery. They were able to cover a lot of ground and were very close to Ben's house now. Not far from his house was a group of old oak trees. Most of them were well over a hundred years old, however, they were spaced fairly far apart, which made it easy to scan the ground. The old road, which had now become a path, was cut in between the grove of the oaks. This was part of the short cut that Christopher and his buddies would take to go swimming in the creek passing by Ben's house during the summer.

To help cover more ground, Christopher would hunt the right side and Paul the left while Ben helped out by removing dead limbs and debris from the area to make it easier to swing the detectors to get as close to the ground as possible. This also made it a much faster process. All in all, all three of the treasure seekers were having a great time and getting more excited by the day just trying to imagine finding a King's ransom in gold coins.

A few days later while hunting near a large rotten stump, Paul received a signal. The object registered as solid iron and seemed to be fairly large. After several passes over the area, he marked it and started to dig. Ben and Christopher were still pre occupied with their own projects and didn't notice Paul had stooped down to dig for the object. Paul finally hit the object with his digger and realized it was larger than he expected but still could not tell what it was. After clearing a larger area of dirt around it, he was able to pull the object out of the ground. Paul proceeded to scrape some of the dirt away from it and then called Christopher and Ben over to see the discovery. "What does this look like to you, Ben?" Paul asked.

Ben took the almost flat piece of iron from Paul to examine it. "I think you may have found what is left of an old shovel." Ben exclaimed. "You still might see a few of these shovel heads around today, but it's been a long time since I have seen one. How long do you think it has been there?" Ben asked.

"That's a good question, but I think it has been there a while, if you see where the handle was attached at one time, it looks like all of that part has rusted away." Paul answered.

Ben placed one hand on his hip and with the other started rubbing his chin. "Now my next question is; what is a shovel head doing buried out here away from everything else? Just maybe it was used to bury something." Ben stated with raised eyebrows.

It was lunchtime and the three marked their stopping point area. They decided to break for lunch and walked to Ben's house to eat and rest on the front porch. It was a beautiful cloudless day with a nice breeze blowing to cool them off. Paul started a conversation after finishing half of his sandwich.

"Men, let's review some things here." He stated. "So far we have found a coin in the barn, and just a few yards up the road here, another identical coin. Now we find what is left of an old shovel. It seems to me things are starting to make more sense here. Let's try to put ourselves in Sam Bailey's shoes that day he robbed the stage coach. Maybe we can trace his steps, if you will, and see if it will lead us closer to the treasure site." Paul stated. Paul finished his sandwich in between his verbal thoughts. "Ben, the other day you brought up a good point about Sam Bailey maybe marking his hiding place with landmarks that would not change over the years, and we have the good fortune of your farm's layout being practically the same since the holdup. My theory is; Sam Bailey robs the stage coach but does not count on getting wounded in the process. His plans changed with that bit of bad luck so he then decides to hide the gold temporarily until he could come back later if he escaped the Sheriff. Maybe he dropped a coin in the barn while trying to find a shovel to bury the gold and dropped another one on his way to the final resting place of the treasure."

Paul leaned back against the pillar on the porch waiting for some opinions from Ben and Christopher enjoying the sandwiches and ice tea. "What do you two think of my theory?" Paul inquired.

Christopher then said. "Dad do you think the shovel you found could be the one he used to dig a hole to hide the gold?"

"I think that could be a very good assumption son." Paul said. "So I think from now on we should even be more diligent in searching every crack and crevasse to make sure we don't miss a thing. I want to be satisfied if we aren't successful in this hunt that the gold is just not there to be found." He added.

Ben drank down a big gulp of tea and proceeded with his take on the situation. "Paul, I agree, after all of the research you have done on this we know for sure that scalawag ancestor of mine did not get any further than my barn. Maybe the coins you and I found were some he took out of the main stash just to have some money for the road so to speak; after all he did not know he was going to get caught and if that was the case he probably didn't know he had some holes in his pockets either; a bad family trait that has apparently been passed down to me." Ben exclaimed.

All three started laughing at Ben's comment. Ben just had a way of saying things that came out funny even though it was mostly unintentional. It was one of the many things people liked about him.

The Old Oak Stump

The treasure hunters finished their lunch and proceeded to take the short hike back to the site where
they found the old shovel head. They were now hunting
at a location that was mostly a wooded area where
many old oak trees had lived a long life before dying
and rotting into thick loose mulch. Paul and Christopher
started scanning the ground again only this time they
were closer together in the oak grove while Ben helped
clear a path for them by removing debris. After about an
hour, Paul noticed his shoelace had come untied. He
had paused near what was left of a huge oak tree. It
must have been at least five feet in diameter and all but
a few blunt remnants of the tree reaching around two

feet tall had rotted to the point of being almost ground level. When viewed from the side it reminded Paul of the skyline of a large city with tall and not so tall buildings. Paul carefully leaned the Gold Duster against the stump with the head of the detector resting against one of the rotting wooden slag's while he bent down to tie his shoe-lace. When he retrieved the detector to get back into hunting position the scanning head accidentally came down close to the soft debris in the middle of the stump. It was then the Gold Duster let out a deep long tone. At first Paul thought he had hit the wrong button to reset the detector for a new start up. Paul raised the scanner head and hit the reset button then lowered it back down to the same place. Again, a deep long tone bellowed out of the machine. Paul looked at the meter. It was resting on the GOLD setting. Paul's thoughts began to race but not nearly as fast as his heart; could this be another coin; in the middle of a stump he thought? Paul repeated the action over and over again even at different loca-tions of the rotted stump. Each time all of the readings came up GOLD. Still bewildered, he took several deep breaths and took off his earphones. He then called to Ben and Christopher to come over. Both ran over to the site with wide eyes. They knew by now through past experiences, Paul would not summon them if it were not a find he thought was important. "Christopher, pass the Little Gold Duster over that spot and see what reading you get." Paul instructed nervously.

Christopher unplugged his earphones and passed the wand over the area. BEEEEEEEEEEEP, BEEEEEEEEEEP sounded out of his machine also. His reading also registered GOLD.

"Dad there is something big under there." He said.

"You're right Son, I know both of our detectors are not giving out false readings." Paul exclaimed. "Let's see if this old tree stump is rotten enough to chip away some of the wood to do a dig." Paul added.

Other than his digger instrument, Paul carried a straight blade hunting knife with an eight-inch blade. He removed it from its sheath and began to slowly and carefully poke the area where the largest reading was coming from. From time to time he would hit an object but it did not feel like a large solid object. The recent spring rains had softened the wood up considerably making it a bit spongy but the longer pieces protruding from the stump were obstructing the effort to remove any rotten center wood from the middle.

After stepping back and studying the problem, Ben came up with an idea. "Let me knock off the taller pieces with my ax. It shouldn't damage what's under there and you will have more room to dig out the softer wood." Ben stated.

"Sounds like our only solution." Paul answered. With the anxious go ahead from Paul and Christopher, Ben got into position to knock the top jagged wood remnants from the stump with his famous snake-killing ax.

"Stand clear men." Ben bellowed, as if he was starting a major tree-chopping project. Ben drew back the ax and swung it hard against the protruding pieces of wood. On his third swing the ax struck the largest deeply embedded jagged piece Ben had targeted. As the ax hit the slag, a large chunk of the stump gave way and completely separated from the main stump. A hidden connected bottom piece of wood went deep into the stump that when struck created a large crater simultaneously flinging uprooted dirt and handfuls of shiny solid gold coins out of the hole on to the rest of the stump and surrounding ground. Before hitting the ground the twirling airborne coins reflected the sun's rays in every direction.

For a brief moment that seemed like eternity it was raining gold coins. After the coins found their final destination, some hurled at least ten feet out, the three hunters stood in frozen amazement just staring at the gaping hole in the stump full of twenty dollar gold pieces, not knowing what to do or say next.

Jackpot

As Paul, Ben and Christopher regained their composure they slowly put down their detectors and Ben his ax then bent down on their knees for a closer look at a sight none of them could believe. Christopher was the first to speak. "Wow Dad, you found the treasure, you found the treasure." He exclaimed.

Paul answered, still trying to take it all in. "No Son, we all found the treasure; we're all three in this hunt together." Ben scanned the sight slowly shaking his head with a big grin on his face while removing a few coins that found a resting place on the top of his hat.

"Gentlemen, I have got to say this is one of the prettiest sights I have seen since I saw my bride walking down the stairs on our wedding day so many years ago. For the first time in my life I am practically speechless, and we all know that is a rare occurrence; this find is truly unbelievable." Ben said shaking his head in amazement.

Ben reached out his hand to Paul and then to Christopher and gave them each a long firm handshake. "Gentlemen, as we regain our composure, I just want to congratulate both of you on your find; your hard work has paid off and even more important factor to me is; you let me be a part of this adventure. I will remember this day and your kindness as long as I live." Ben exclaimed.

Paul leaned back, thought for a moment then responded to Ben's toast. He then realized Ben really did not care as much about the gold discovery as he did about their friendship. Paul hesitated a moment, then responded to Ben.

"Ben, you do realize this gold belongs to you, not to us. As far as I'm concerned this is your property, this is your treasure and as of this moment you are a very rich man Mr. Bailey." Paul exclaimed smiling and laughing. Ben just smiled shook his head and put his dirty hand on Paul's shoulder. "Paul as far as I'm concerned, I became a rich man when I met you and your family, that means more to an old man like me than all the gold in the world." Paul would never forget Benjamin Bailey's words that day.

A Close Call

*A*fter regaining their composer, Paul, Ben and Christopher began the pain staking task of removing the treasure from the stump, which was not going to be easy, as many of the coins were imbedded in the tree roots. Even though the stump was totally rotten they had a difficult and tedious job ahead of them. At one point Paul pulled up a root that had coins embedded out of it from all sides resembling a crude Christmas tree covered with gold ornaments. While picking the stubborn coins out of the roots Paul stopped for a moment.

"Ben I still cannot understand how a tree could absorb coins like this, I am at a total loss to understand how this could happen. "Paul stated scratching his head. Ben stopped his chore also and paused for a moment in thought.

"Paul it's funny you said that as not only a few minutes ago I was trying to figure that out myself. Then I remembered something from my very early days here. There was an old tree here we use to call the V Tree. We called it that because it was shaped like a big V. Now here is the interesting part, the tree had a hollow hole in the middle where the two large branches separated. All of the kids back then were scared to even look into it thinking there were snakes and such hiding in there. What do you think the chances are that scalawag got short on time and just threw those bags of gold down that hollow hole?"

Paul's face lit up just listening to Ben's story. "Ben, that has to be it that is the only explanation. It was a quick hiding place and the tree shape was a perfect landmark to return to. I think you have solved another mystery here Ben." Paul exclaimed cheerfully.

"Just glad I could help Son." Ben said smiling. Paul sent Christopher to the truck parked on the ridge to retrieve a large bucket. The excited Christopher ran to get the bucket. When he reached the truck he could see two figures on bicycles coming toward him. It was Sam and Monte undoubtedly looking for Christopher to play, as it had been a while since they had gotten together due to his gold fever adventure. Christopher grabbed the bucket and ran down to Paul and Ben as fast as he could. "Dad, Dad, Mr. Ben, Sam and Monte are coming up the road." He cried.

Paul immediately responded. "Quick, we can't let them see this; they will tell the whole county what we found."

Ben got puzzled look on his face, then suddenly understanding what Paul meant, he immediately took charge.

"Paul, you and Chris go stall them at the truck, I'll get some brush and leaves and cover this old stump up until they leave." Ben stated.

"Good thinking Ben." Paul exclaimed. "We'll be back when they are safely gone then I will explain why we must keep this discovery a secret at all cost."Sam and Monte reached the truck and made some small talk with Christopher. When they found out he might be helping Ben clear some brush and debris they quickly smelled it might be some work involved interfering with their plans and scurried away on their bikes.

"That was close." Paul said. He and Christopher waited until the two boys were long gone and made their way back to the gold filled stump. Ben was waiting with a big grin on his face after figuring out what was going on."I owe you a detailed explanation of my actions Ben." Paul exclaimed.

"Oh not really Paul; I think I know at least some of the reasons why we need to keep this historical find top secret and I don't blame you." Ben answered.

Paul and Christopher sat down next to the stump for a brief rest in relief of the last few moments. They had worked up a good double sweat and their hearts were still pounding with excitement.

"Ben, this is the way I see it and tell me if you agree or disagree." Paul replied. "You see, some treasure hunters are not very courteous when it comes to respecting people's property especially when they think there is gold to be found."

"What do you mean, Dad?" Christopher asked. "Well Son, I can only tell you and Ben a true story that happened a few years ago to give you an example of my concern." Paul replied.

"Not long ago, a couple of treasure hunters discovered some buried coins in jars a couple of counties west of here on an elderly couples land. And mind you these were not even gold coins. It turns out that the word got out fairly quick on their discovery of many rare silver coins buried by the owner's grandfather many years before. This was a great discovery and made the news not only in the state but also nationwide in the treasure hunting circles. After the discovery the couple living there was inundated with strangers stopping by to look for more treasure. It was so many people the couple started refusing to let people on their land. Totally ignoring the couples request, undesirables started sneaking in at night digging holes everywhere and finally someone broke into their home and tore up everything they could get their hands on, looking for treasure. Thankfully the elderly couple was not there at the time. My point is; this helped to ruin their lives because of the discovery of coins in a jar on their land. You can only imagine if the word got around what we have found here it would spread like wildfire to every county and probably to the surrounding states that there was even more treasure on Ben's property; it would be a nightmare not to mention the non-treasure hunters that are just plain thieves. It could even mean Mr. Ben's life could be threatened and could change life as we know it in Summerville for a long time." Paul finished.

Ben nodded his head in agreement. "You know Son you're absolutely right and I appreciate you thinking this out cause I sure haven't; it's sad the world is turning cold like that but it is a fact and I totally agree. It's a shame though, I was hoping you could get your picture in that treasure hunting magazine you let me borrow and be famous cause this is the find of a lifetime." Ben exclaimed.

Paul paused and answered after digesting Ben's statement. He had not thought about the magazine yet. He had to admit to himself that was a disappointment. But he did not let it show to the others.

"I appreciate your kind intentions Ben, but your safety and the wellbeing of our town is much more important to me." Paul answered. "Now, let's get to work and figure out how we are going to get the rest of these coins out of this stump; we are running out of daylight."

A King's Ransom

After verifying the coast was clear a second time, all three-treasure hunters began to carefully remove the beautiful gold coins from the stump to the large bucket. Paul instructed Ben and Christopher to be sure to be on the lookout for anything else that might have been consumed by the large oak which Ben had already nicknamed the "treasure oak."

"Just think, Ben said; as a little boy I must have played around and climbed this old oak thousands of times and right under my nose was a King's Ransom in gold. Life is very strange when you really take time to think about it."

"What do you mean Mr. Ben?" Christopher inquired.

"Well Chris, just think about it from the beginning, how we met, how your Dad found the old newspapers in the secret room with no other copies in existence, and just a few hours ago how he put his metal detector down to simply tie his shoe and, "WHALLA," we are putting old gold coins in a bucket; this is still a miracle to me." Ben answered.

Paul stopped for a moment and looked at Ben as if a light had been turned on in his head.

"You know Ben, you're absolutely right, in all of this excitement I haven't even taken time to realize how true your words are. Everything has fallen into place almost like we were lead here. I would have never thought to run the Gold Duster across this old rotten stump in a million years."

"Maybe God helped us find the treasure." Christopher piped in.

Ben and Paul both leaned back resting on their knees looked at each other with Ben the first to reply. "Chris, I think you are probably the most insightful and brilliant little guy I have ever met and I think you are one hundred per cent right, God did lead us to this treasure and I don't think our adventure has ended yet even though we have found it." Ben replied.

Paul looked puzzled for a moment while Ben continued.

"Chris you don't realize this but you have given me answers to some very important questions that have been running through this old brain of mine since these coins jumped out at us. When we get all of this treasure secured, me, you and your father are going to have a long talk about it's future. "Although Paul had no idea what Ben was talking about he had learned Ben was a planner and never did anything half way no matter what it was, so he was curious and looking forward to hearing Ben's plan.

Although they did not take time to count the coins, it was a good thing that the bucket was a large one as it was about a third full when the dig was complete and quite heavy. Paul and Christopher scanned the stump and the surrounding area one more time just to make sure they had retrieved every gold piece.

Paul commented. "This is amazing. When Samuel Bailey hid this gold, he probably used this tree as a marker to return back to when the heat was off; when that plan was spoiled this old oak just kept growing and growing and surrounded the gold in the process. This whole thing is still unreal to me, I have never heard of such a discovery of this caliber being found in the middle of a two hundred year old tree. It's almost like she protected it for us until it was time to be discovered."

Paul put his hand on Christopher's shoulder and gave him a multiple loving pat only a father could do."Your absolutely right Son, God did lead us to this treasure, and I for one can't wait to find out why."

Counting The Loot

Paul and Ben rode back to Ben's house with Christopher hitching a ride in the back of the truck. It was a short drive but long enough for Ben to explain to Paul some future plans for the treasure if it turned out to be possible for him to keep it. Ben came up with a great idea of having only the people that were aware of the possibility of gold being hidden some-where, to have a group meeting. Ben did not have time to fully explain his idea before they pulled up in front of his house. "I'll go into some more details later. For now I think we need to find a safe place for this treasure and review just what we have here." Ben remarked.

Paul agreed and they took the bucket of coins into Ben's house. The three started to transfer the coins from the bucket to the old kitchen table in counting them in the process. All of the coins had the same date and mint on them, another fact convincing Paul these had to be the stolen stagecoach gold pieces. It was obvious they had never been circulated and looked as new as the day they were minted."What do you think these coins are worth in today's market?' Ben asked.

"I really don't know Ben, it probably depends on how rare they might be; but I have been thinking, with your permission I would like to take one or two with me next week when I make my rounds in the city to call on my customers; I have a good friend there who is an antique and coin collector and very trustworthy to keep quiet. He could probably tell me exactly what they are worth." Paul replied.

"That is an outstanding idea Paul; feel free to take whatever you need, after all I believe this is just as much yours and Chris's treasure than it is mine. When you get back from your trip, I want to have a meeting with a few folks in town to discuss a plan I have; I'll give you the details then, to see what you think of it."

"Sounds like a good idea. I believe I will stop by my parent's house on the way home and inform them on the great find. This still seems like a dream to me Ben; I don't think I have fully grasped the magnitude of what we have discovered." Paul replied. "Well don't feel like the Lone Ranger Paul cause I feel the same way. Do you realize we have almost three hundred gold coins here; it's unreal what this treasure might be worth, I can't wait for you to talk to your friend in the city Paul." Ben replied.

"Me either Ben; me either. "Paul said.

Christopher put the last coin on the table and interjected. "That's the last one Dad; you think we can eat now, I'm hungry?"

The Coin Collector

*P*aul left the next morning to make his business rounds taking two gold coins with him. He was going to try to meet with a very prominent coin collector and longtime friend Mark Corrigan. Paul had met Mark years ago in college. The two found out they shared the same interest in history and just about everything else and became the very best of friends. Mark had visited Paul's hometown many times during their college years and his passion for collecting old and rare coins had developed into a lucrative career. He finally realized his dream of opening up a small shop in the big city specializing in some of the most rare coins and memorabilia in the world. When in the area on business,

Paul would always stop in to see Mark to check on him and just take in the history of objects of rarity Mark had acquired over the years. Mark loved to hear what was going on in Paul's life and the first thing he would say when Paul came through the door.

"Well, have you found that illusive gold coin yet?"

Paul would always shake his head and answer.

"Not yet, but I'm not giving up my friend." Then the two would each have a hearty laugh and shake hands and discuss bygone college days while catching up on the latest news in both of their worlds. This visit was to be very different. Paul entered the shop only to see his friend behind a glass case examining one of his latest acquisitions with a magnifying glass. As the door opened it tripped a small bell on the top of the door facing alerting Mark of customers entering. The little shop had a smorgasbord mixture of old and new items with an aroma of old cedar with a hint of mothballs. There was hardly a square inch of wall or counter space that wasn't covered with something unusual from old toys to beautiful paintings. Most of the display cases were full of old coins. The building itself was about as old or older as most of items that were on display.Paul had planned this visit out very carefully and he was going to enjoy it. Mark looked up and asked Paul the same age-old question he had asked for years.

"Well old friend have you found that illusive gold coin yet?" Mark mused with a slight chuckle.

Paul walked up to the antique glass case that separated them and gently but firmly put a shiny gold coin on the mauve velvet cloth on top of the case.

"Does this answer your question; ole friend?" Paul replied.

Mark stopped and stared a few seconds before picking up the coin.

"Well, well, well, you finally put that old metal detector to good use, what did you do, change the batteries? Now, what do have we here?" Mark replied in a snidely manner.

"Something I hope you are going to like and can help me with." Paul jokingly quipped. As Mark looked a little more closely at the coin Paul noticed a very curious look on his face. A look he could not decipher as good or bad; a look he had never seen on his old friend's face. Mark scrambled for his magnifying glass nervously cleaning with small strokes with a piece of cheese cloth looking intently at the coin turning it over and over. He seemed to get more excited each time he examined it. Then in a totally serious business voice as if Paul was a total stranger; he started quizzing him.

"Paul, May I ask where you got this, did you find it or buy it, where did this coin come from, seriously?" Mark asked in an almost demanding way.

"Well, I found it with the help of that old metal detector you keep making fun of." Paul answered in a cool manner, enjoying every minute of his friend's reaction. Paul was enjoying toying with his friend not realizing the revelation he was getting ready to hear. Then, in very short and to the point interrupting inquiry Mark asked."Paul, can I hold this coin and do some research on it; how long are you going to be in town?" Mark desperately inquired.

"Well, sure, I guess, I was going to ask you if we could have dinner tonight at our favorite Italian restaurant and catch up on things." Paul answered.

Mark paused for a couple of seconds still intently examing the coin, hardly looking up at Paul."That's perfect; it will give me enough time to get you some reliable information on your find." Mark answered.

"Great, is 7:30 ok?" Paul asked.

"I will see you then and don't be late we have much to talk about." Mark instructed.

Paul left the shop somewhat bewildered, but before he went out the front door he turned to give Mark a final wave of goodbye. Mark had already opened two coin books and was nervously turning the pages almost in a panic and never heard Paul's words. Paul left shaking his head in satisfaction and curiosity of what had just transpired looking forward to their dinner.

Unbelievable

Paul arrived at the restaurant just a few minutes early and was surprised to find Mark had already arrived. Before Paul could even tell the owner who was seating the guest what party he was meeting, he was met with "Oh yes, Mr. Taylor; Mr. Corrigan is in our special private room in the back and is expecting you; please follow me."

Paul laughed to himself as Mark had never had them sit in a private room, if fact, Paul did not even know there was a private dining room in the back. Yes, something was brewing and Paul was curious to find out just what. When they reached the private room Mark seemed very anxious to see Paul but had grown more relaxed.

"Well Paul, how was your meetings today?" He asked.

"Oh they were great; I even finished early and was surprised you were here already." Paul answered.

"Well I just wanted to make sure we could have some privacy because I have some very good news for you on your coin and it is something I did not need for people to overhear." Mark replied in a slightly lower voice. "Good news, that's great I can always use that." Paul replied. The waiter then came and the two friends ordered their meal and returned to the conversation. Making sure the waiter had left completely, Mark pulled the gold coin from his pocket. He had placed it in a plastic transparent display cover to protect it and gave it to Paul.

"This little cover is nice, I appreciate it Mark. So you said you have some good news for me?"

Mark leaned back in his plush seat. "Boy do I; after you left, I closed the shop and did some research on this little beauty, it seems you have found one of the rarest gold coins ever made in America, even the world. This particular coin was very limited in production as it was minted incorrectly and is a collectors dream. Very few exist. I have only seen one in the flesh in my whole career and it was owned by a multi-millionaire and the word is even he had a hard time and spent a lot of money to secure it for his collection." Paul took a deep breath and leaned back in his chair. He could not believe what he was hearing.

Mark continued. "I would say you did good on this one, it might have taken you a long time but when you finally found your illusive gold coin, you found the best ole buddy." Mark said.

"So, this is one of the rarest gold coins in existence?" Paul repeated.

"That's right; you have got yourself a chunk of money here Paul, a very nice investment. I would offer to buy it from you but I couldn't afford to pay you, something like this would have to go on a private auction if you ever wanted to sell it." Mark said.

The food was now starting to be served and the two made small talk for a while until they had their privacy again. Between conversation Paul was still trying to grasp the news.

"Mark, I have something else to show you." Paul reached into his vest pocket and pulled out a second coin and handed it to Mark.

"Holy Jackpot." Mark halfway shouted when he saw it the second coin. "You mean there is a Mr. and Mrs. Liberty; this is unbelievable, two of them." Mark replied. Paul laughed and said. "I hope the owners don't mind how long we stay because I have a long story to tell you; my friend. One you are going to find hard to believe."

"Well, you know me and you know I love a good story; and don't leave out a single detail no matter how long it takes to tell it; we will just have to close down the place for Mario and have an extra dessert and deplete his coffee supply." Mark replied.

After stressing the importance of secrecy and the reason for it to Mark, Paul proceeded to relay the greatest adventure he had ever participated in to his friend while finishing up the delicious meal. Many times Paul could tell Mark wanted to interrupt with questions but he was able to restrain himself. Paul relayed everything from Ben Bailey saving his son's life, the secret room with the old newspapers, the stage robbery all up to the big finale of the discovery of the complete treasure. When Paul reached the part where they dug up the treasure, Mark could no longer contain himself and just had to interrupt Paul's story.

"Wait, Wait, Wait, hold on just one minute Paul; you mean to tell me that there is a whole cache of uncirculated gold coins that match these two beauties?" Mark inquired.

Paul, who was getting a big kick out of playing it cool, calmly answered. "Oh yeah, I guess I forgot to mention that; I would say we have around two hundred and fifty so far." Paul answered.

Mark laid his fork down and leaned back in the fancy high back chair with a dumb founded look as the blood left his face.

"Paul, do you realize these coins are worth millions at private auction and are probably the last that exist in the world?" He repeated. "I can sell as many as I can get my hands on and practically name the price; and how you found them sounds like something right out of one of those mystery adventure movies." Mark cried.

"I know, I can still hardly believe it myself; and it's good to know you will have little trouble selling some of the coins because I'm not sure what the owner is planning to do with them, but I have a feeling we will probably be calling you for your professional services soon." Paul answered.

"I still can't believe this; does your friend realize what these coins are worth?" Mark repeated. "To tell you the truth Mark, I didn't realize the scope of this discovery until now and it is still hard for me to grasp it and in some ways it makes me slightly nervous. But I'm sure the owner will make a very rational decision as to the treasure's future."Paul replied.

"Well Paul, you know where I am; just give me the word and I can take care of things for you very indiscreetly I might add." Mark answered.

"Thank you Mark, I knew I could depend on you; however you have brought up something I haven't thought about." Paul answered.

"What's that?" Mark asked.

"Well considering the rarity of these coins and their worth, might this possibly put you in danger if the word gets out to the public, I mean, I wouldn't what a bunch of thieves coming in and threatening you to give up your source or anything of that nature." Paul said.

Mark set his excitement of the discovery aside while rubbing his chin and began to ponder what Paul had just said.

"Paul that is a good point but don't worry about me I will only sell these for you at very exclusive private auctions; these guys that bid on these rare items are super private millionaires and a few are billionaires; your secret and my safety will be secure." Mark answered.

"Good, that makes me feel much better." Paul answered.

"Now on another subject; is the fishing in Summerville as good as it was when we were boys?" Mark inquired.

"It's even better." Paul answered.

"I'm way overdue to come back down there and visit my adopted second home town to see everyone and just get out of this rat race for a while; the older I get the more I miss the good small town life, you're a lucky guy Paul, and smart for not letting the lure of the big city keep you out of your little town." Mark said.

"Well the good thing is; Angela and I have plenty of room for you and our home is yours anytime you want to come home to visit, or, even stay." Paul answered.

Mark hesitated and acquired a slightly sad look in his eyes. He seemed to be reminiscing about his boyhood days just for a fleeting few seconds. He then answered Paul.

"My good friend; you have no idea how good that makes me feel hearing those words." Mark exclaimed.

"There's something I need to leave you with Mark, before we finish here tonight. "Paul said.

Paul reached into his pocket and pulled out the first gold coin he had ever found and pushed it across the table to Mark.

"Oh, you want me to auction one for you already my friend?" Mark joked while smiling. Paul looked at his old friend square in his eyes.

"No my friend, this coin is for you to keep." Paul answered.

Mark had a look of shock on his face. "Man, I can't accept this, do you know what this is worth? I mean, I can take a little commission from selling them for you, but Paul; this is too much." Mark answered.

"I want you to have it Mark, in a way it will make you part of our future organization I told you about tonight, and I promise you will probably earn every penny of what it is worth by helping us." Paul said.

Mark stared at the gift Paul had just given in amazement. "Thank you Paul this is still too much and I am speechless; there is one downside to this though." Mark replied in a serious manner.

"And what is that?" Paul asked.

Mark started to laugh. "Now I can't rib you anymore about wandering around those hills searching for that illusive gold coin; I'm going to have to find another subject to bust your chops on when you stop by."

Paul laughed out loud. "And for that fact my friend, this gift is worth more than any amount of gold to me." Paul answered while raising his glass.The two friends finished the meal and after some more small talk and laughter left the restaurant late that night both feeling very good about the meeting agreeing to meet the next time Paul came to town or when Mark would visit Summerville.

Mark drove Paul to the train station. As they parted, Mark would always leave Paul with his famous parting words to his ole friend.

"Keep your powder dry my man." Mark said, smiling ear to ear.

"You do the same ole friend; and don't take any wooden gold coins." Returned Paul.

As Paul's train pulled out of the station, his thoughts were a mixed bag of future plans for the treasure, the coming meeting with Ben and hopefully his college friend coming to Summerville. This time maybe to stay for good.

The Secret Club

After returning from his business trip Paul wasted no time contacting Ben to tell him what he had learned about the treasure. Ben was very pleased and Paul had a feeling he had decided exactly what to do with the gold. Ben told Paul while he was on his trip that he also had a meeting with Paul's cousin Walton. Ben had retained Walton as his lawyer for some other legal matters and instantly liked him both professionally and personally. Ben informed Paul he had not spilled the beans on their discovery but he did run some "what if" questions by Walton. Ben then asked Paul if he had time to talk; he wanted to see what he thought of his plan.

"Sure Ben, I am actually anxious to hear the details your plan." Paul answered. "Paul, the first part of my plan is to bring all of the folks that know about the gold hunt together here for a meeting." Ben said.

Ben then proceeded to explain what else he had in mind for the get together. "Can you help me contact all of these folks?" Ben asked. "I would be glad to Ben." Paul answered.

"Paul you are the man for this job because I know how strongly you feel about keeping this discovery secret at all cost." Ben stated.

A meeting date was agreed upon and Paul and Ben invited the list of people who would attend. Everyone they contacted was curious as they knew nothing of the discovery of the treasure but they sensed Paul and Christopher had been looking for something big for a long time. It was a Thursday night when everyone met at Ben's house at seven o'clock. Ben held the meeting in the parlor. All of the homes original furniture was still there. Ben had a beautiful round mahogany table located in the middle of the room, which was directly under an antique chandelier that provided ample light for the enormous area. An exact number of chairs had been placed around the table. He had placed a cardboard box in the middle of the table with the closed side facing up hiding the content under it very well. He also had made some of his famous chocolate chip cookies and had other refreshments for his guest. Paul, Angela and Christopher were the first to arrive and seeing the setup were very curious as to what Ben had in mind. Of course it did not take long for Christopher's curiosity to get the best of him so he had to ask;

"What's under that box Mr. Ben?"

Ben knew it was coming and gave out a hearty laugh. "I was wondering who was going to be the first to ask, but have patience Chris I am going to answer everyone's questions very soon tonight. Besides you are already very familiar with the contents." He answered with a wink. The other guests soon arrived and were directed to the parlor. They included Aunt Evelyn, her daughter

Joyce, Walton Griffin and Paul's father and mother and the town's Pastor, Robert Major. Paul and Angela had secured a baby sitter for Arielle and Alyssa as they had no idea how long the meeting would last, they knew the two little girls would either sleep or whine through it if they attended. After everyone was seated and had enjoyed some small talk, Ben rose from his chair and asked for everyone's attention.

"Well folks I know you are curious about this little get together and I want to start off by saying how much I appreciate all of you coming here tonight. This is a very informal meeting and I will try not to keep you very long as I have a feeling when I finish many of you will have some questions. As you see I have a box on the table covering something I believe to be a God send for everyone in our town. I would like to show it to you now and explain why we are here tonight." Ben stated.

Ben leaned over the old table and carefully lifted the cardboard box straight up not disturbing what was under it. When the box was removed it revealed stacks and stacks of gold coins. Ben had meticulously stacked the coins in slightly uneven towers just to show off the beauty of the treasure. The overhead light intensified the coins sparkle even more, like diamonds in a case under the lights in a fine jewelry store. As he presented the treasure the room grew quiet just for a fleeting second until everyone realized what they were witnessing. It sent shivers over the onlookers who remained oddly quiet as Ben continued his speech. "Isn't this one of the most beautiful sights you have ever laid your eyes on?" Ben asked.

"Even if you are not a treasure hunter you have to be impressed." He said.

The gatherers began to talk among themselves for a few seconds; all were still in awe of what they were witnessing. A few excited questions were asked and were answered promptly. Ben waited for a minute then proceeded. "I know you all have questions about the coins on the table and I promise either myself, Paul or Chris will be glad to answer them directly. But first I want to tell you all why I asked you here tonight and ultimately ask for your help with something that is very dear to my heart; especially now, thanks to Paul and Chris's perseverance with finding these beautiful and rare coins." Ben said.

Ben paused for a moment to gather his thoughts then relayed one of the most heartfelt and sincere revelations Paul had ever heard. "Folks when I came back to Summerville, my plan was to live out the rest of my days just trying to get by in this life, not asking for anything or bothering anyone. Well, it looks like the Good Lord had another plan for me; and I give thanks to him every day for giving me the sense to realize it. He did that by allowing me to meet Paul Taylor and his beautiful loving family. They, because of their Christian prayers and unselfish kindness, helped reintroduce me to the Good Lord and the lovely and giving people of Summerville. The love and kindness I have been shown here can never be compared in worth to a whole room full of gold coins; it is something a man cannot put a value on because it is the greatest of all gifts we can give to each other. All of you in this room are to thank for that; you are the finest people I have ever met and I want to say again; Thank You from the bottom of a formally bitter and lost old man's heart."

Ben then paused. "Some of you are aware of how this treasure came to be here, it started out by being stolen from the stage coach line over a hundred years ago by what appears to be one of my thieving ancestors that took a wrong turn somewhere down the road of life."

The group could tell Ben was having a hard time dealing with Sam Bailey's sin when his voice would crack while explaining the details of the adventure. One could not tell if the reason was due to sadness or anger at what Sam Bailey had done. It was probably a little of both.

Ben continued. "Tagging along with Paul and Chris on this treasure hunt has been one of the most, if not the most memorable and enjoyable times in my twilight years. I will never forget this great adventure. When those gold coins popped out of that old oak stump it was like the old tree was saying; finally, someone has found my treasure that I have been guarding all of these years; I can now rest in peace, make sure you make this treasure count for something Benjamin Bailey. Now, I know that probably sounds silly to most of you but it was at that moment I realized if I was allowed to keep this treasure I knew exactly what to do with it. I have discussed the legal ownership matters of this gold with Mr. Griffin here and he has informed me".

Ben then paused for a brief moment. "You know folks, I think you need to hear from Mr. Griffin here on the official report of the gold's owner ship, so I am going to give him the floor for a few words." Ben stated.

Walton Griffin, looking somewhat surprise, stood to address the group. He pressed a few fingers deep in his vest pocket with his left hand and with his right hand clamped on to his jacket lapel tightly with his thumb and forefinger just as if he was presenting a case before a jury. Then took a deep breath. "Folks, Mr. Bailey and I have gone over the circumstances of this rare find from where the treasure originated from to the discovery a few weeks ago. It seems to me and the law, at least the law in Summerville according to the Griffin Law Firm, that this find should be treated like a lost wallet or maybe a misplaced piece of jewelry. As of this meeting we have had no one record any document that they have lost a gold coin much less almost three hundred of them. So, my official opinion on this matter is. Finders Keepers, Losers Weepers. This gold belongs to Benjamin Bailey to do with it as he sees fit."

Walton Griffin had just proven his sense of humor was still very much alive as he returned to his seat with tongue in cheek while the whole group was laughing out loud.

Ben, still laughing and trying to maintain his composure rose to finish his talk on his plan for the fortune.

"Folks I really appreciate Mr. Griffin clearing up the legalities for us in this matter. Now this is where I need all of you to help me. What Sam Bailey stole, Ben Bailey is going to give back. You see, I believe this treasure belongs to the people of this town and with your help I intend on giving it back to them. In my opinion the people of this town are the true treasures of Summerville. I will say it again, make no mistake about it, the Good Lord allowed us to find this treasure for a reason." Ben said. Some of the group surrounding the table were smiling in approval while there was even a trace of a tear in a few eyes but all said and done everyone overwhelmingly approved of Ben's opinion. Ben then proceeded to explain where their help would be needed and how important they all were if this plan was to succeed; they were all now even more curious and were starting to hang on every word he spoke.

Ben explained "Since I have returned back to town I have been getting reacquainted with everyone and I have noticed there are many proud people here that resist any kind of outside help unless they can't possibly make it anymore. For example, Bob Stewart has lost two crops of corn here lately; most of Tom Matthew's cattle herd died before they could catch the disease to implement a cure; that's not to mention Ms. Wiley, whose husband was sick and passed away leaving her with doctor bills she can't pay; then there's Matt and Jessica Lott whose little girl is very sick and they do not have a reliable vehicle for the trip to see the doctor; we all know the list goes on and on and these are just a few of our town mates that are too proud to accept help. Why, most of these families are direct descendants of the same families of the time period when this gold was stolen. We all know there is only so much we can do with our talents on assisting folks but sometimes the bottom line is; it just takes money to help out. This is why I asked you here tonight; I want all of you to be my eyes and ears on situations of our townsfolk that need assistance; in short I want you to spy for me."

Ben laughed.

The whole room laughed with Ben but understood exactly what he was saying; everyone thought it was the kindest idea anyone could have. Ben continued with details of his plan and stressed the reason and importance of secrecy in executing it.

Ben continued. "The way I see it; we have a perfect situation here. Everyone here sees a different group of people every day; for example, Aunt Evelyn and Joyce talk to people at the General Store, we all know one can get more news there than in a Beauty Parlor on Saturday morning. Angela talks to people at her shop and the Library; Chris can handle the school front through his buddies."

Christopher sported a big smile on his face upon hearing that. It made him feel more grown up and important. This was a fact that Ben was acutely aware of and took every opportunity to stress to others about his little friend. "Brother Major here talks to people needing help every day, and JB could cover the ranch and farming front needs. This group would have just about every angle of need covered in town." Ben said. Ben informed the group that Paul was in charge of transferring the coins into dollars and would secretly award anyone in need in cash money. The master plan was for them to report the need to Ben, Paul or Walton, then money would be secured and either show up in a mailbox or doorstep or any other safe and secure place which would include a special letter to the needy family. After spending a few more minutes explaining the details of the plan, Ben got everyone's attention once more. "Everyone, before we adjourn tonight, I have something for each of you."

Ben had put one coin in the extra plastic covers given to Paul by Mark Corrigan, one for each person in the secret group. He handed each one of them a gold coin.

"This is a way of saying thank you for what you are about to do and to remind us we are all one group; a club if you will, I am not going to use one penny of this treasure for myself but I do have a few more plans for some of it for a few choice projects that are very important that I care about deeply. Thank you all for coming tonight and I hope this is just the beginning of a long giving relationship." Ben finished.

After several more meetings and excellent suggestions from everyone on how to execute the secret gifts to the needy recipients of the town, the group decided they needed a name for the organization. To the surprise of no one, especially Paul and Ben, at one meeting Christopher blurted out how this was like Christmas time every day. That statement stuck in Ben's mind and he suggested that they should just refer to their organization as the "Everyday Christmas Club" with only the club members knowing the name. They would refer to it as the ECC for short. Ben made it a point to thank his buddy Chris in the next meeting for his fine suggestion. As Christopher grew older he would realize how important these acts of kindness were. This would be another chapter of Christopher Taylor starting to grow up on his way to true manhood and responsibility. The gift plan worked flawlessly, the chosen recipients would find money in places that only they would routinely visit every day. The money would always include an unsigned personal letter written by Angela Taylor with an explanation that this was a gift from the town of unnamed persons and was not to be repaid under any circumstances. It also politely asked the recipients to try to refrain from finding out who the giver of monies were. Angela came up with the brilliant idea of using the old typewriter found in the secret room to type the letters preventing anyone recognizing her handwriting.

Everyone in the ECC organization received the greatest satisfaction in giving and being a part of Ben's club. There would be many recipients in the years to follow.

In the months that followed hardly a word was ever spoken from any of the recipients who the club had chosen except for one particular Sunday morning after the 11:00 service. When Pastor Major asked if there were any special prayer needs or praises of answered prayer, a one Seth Thompson slowly rose to his feet to speak. Seth had been through some very difficult days of family sickness with his daughter, Jenny, who was not expected to live. Everyone was surprised when he stood to speak, as Seth was one of the shyer and quieter fellows in town, Seth was not a complainer and would never ask for help. Through water filled eyes and trembling lips, Seth began to speak.

"Folks, I don't know who it is or what the name is of this angel of mercy that left us a gift a few days ago, but I have a feeling they are sitting in this room with us now. And, and, I just want to say, God Bless You. Me and my family so appreciate and love you for what you have done. Jenny is responding to this new treatment now and is on the road to recovery. God has met our need through your kindness. I know the note that we got says not to thank anyone."

Seth then broke down in uncontrollable tears.

"But, but, there are just no words that have been invented to express my thanks to whoever you are. Your gift has helped to save my little girls life."

Seth then sat down by his wife and family to the sound of several "AMENS" and sobs from the congregation. All of the club members were attending church service that morning and did a good job of acting clueless on Seth Thompson's revelation. No words were every exchanged of the incident among themselves but it was safe to say they all had a very warm and satisfied feeling inside with the success of their endeavor, especially the three treasure hunters.

All Aboard

Just a few months later, a terrible rumor that if proven true would be a disaster for the town of Summerville, started circulated around town. It seemed the private company that owned and operated the Number 2 Engine Railway Company that supplied the town with most of its supplies and travel, was to be shut down at the end of the year with even the tracks being pulled up for scrap metal sales. When the town's Mayor and the city council verified that the rumor was indeed true, needless to say, all of the citizens, especially the business owners were very concerned. They knew their town would die a slow and painful death if this came to pass as there were hardly any other companies that ran supply trucks to Summerville. Businesses that had been passed down from generation to generation would close, prices would rise to the farmers and ranchers, and many folks especially the elderly would not be able to adapt to such a drastic change. Mayor Jack Wiggins called a special emergency town meeting with all citizens urged to attend; something in all of his years as Mayor he had never had to do.

Mayor Wiggins was a short robust man with a heart as big as the ocean. He deeply loved the citizens of his hometown. He was born and raised in a small farm house just outside of town and had lived there for all of his fifty three years. His main occupation was accounting when not fulfilling the Mayoral duties, where he had an upstairs office on the town square just above the Farmer's Hardware store. He had been the Mayor for many terms and the people of Summerville had no notion of ever letting him retire from that position. The Mayor had never been this concerned for the future of his town in his whole life.

A Friday evening was picked for the town meeting. It appeared the whole town had indeed shown up to hear the straight of the matter with many citizens having to take their place outside the building. The large eight foot tall windows were raised to the top to create a cross breeze in the crowded town hall. Ben Bailey as well as Paul and Angela Taylor managed to arrive in time to secure a seat on the back row. Mayor Wiggins called the meeting to order after asking Ms Emily Holt to take the minutes. The Mayor calmly explained the facts of what he knew about the situation, talking about fifteen minutes. After he finished, he paused to let the upset citizens quiet down, and then continued.

"Ladies and Gentlemen, I have told you all I know on this important matter, now, I would like to open up this meeting for your suggestions and ideas on how we can save our train; but before I do, I would like for us to bow our heads in prayer."

Everyone quietly and quickly bowed their heads while the Mayor led them in prayer.

[Our most Gracious Heavenly Father; we thank you for all of the blessings you have bestowed on our grateful citizens; we have gathered here tonight to ask for your perfect guidance in this desperate matter. Lord, we ask that you reveal an answer to our plight in the hearts and minds of your servants and give us a solution that is in your will. We trust you Lord and we love you Lord, all that we have is because of you. We ask this in your loving and holy name. Amen.]

The floor now was open for any ideas and suggestions all being recorded in the minutes. Many suggestions were offered that night but after a few had been listened to, one suggestion seemed to stand out in popularity more than the others, and started a chain reaction of comments. "Why don't we pool our money and buy the railroad ourselves?" Came a comment from the crowd.

"You know, I had a good crop this year, I can pitch in some money." Came a comment from another citizen.

"Well, beef prices were low for me this year, but I am more than willing to give what I have to save our train." Came another comment from the crowd.

But, when a certain hand was raised in the middle of the room for permission to speak, an instant hush covered the room like a blanket. The man was Stewart Maitland, a native of Summerville, a friend of everyone, especially the ranchers and farmers of the valley. After Maitland returned from the war he settled back into his home town as a Structural Engineer. But, he had rather be called an Inventor, as he had dedicated his talents to helping the ranchers and farmers troubleshoot daily equipment problems by inventing new designs for their ranching and farming needs. They would simply show him their problem and it was a safe bet Stewart Maitland would come up with a better and easier way to do the chore. Mayor Wiggins gave Stewart Maitland the floor.

"Folks, everyone here knows I am no public speaker by any means, but I feel this needs to be addressed. I agree we need to save the ole No. 2 for our businesses and such, but I have even more personal reasons for saving her. I feel that an even more important factor would be the history and legacy that would be forever lost and forgotten if she was scrapped. If you think about it, I'm sure every old timer here, like me, has a special memory of her. My warmest memory is the day I came home from the war. Many veterans here tonight know the terrible things we witnessed never knowing if we would live to see the sunset much less ever come back home. Well, I will never forget that day, that wonderful day I was coming home on the No.2. The train had come around the last stretch of mountains and I saw my home town again after two years. There on the dock was my wife and parents to welcome me home. About a half a mile out from town, the ole No.2 blew her whistle to announce we were arriving. I can tell you that was the most beautiful sound I had ever heard. To this day every time I hear that whistle I thank God he brought me home safe to my family, my friends, my home town. Now, that whistle serves to remind me of my blessings.

I think, without the No. 2, NO; I know, without the No 2, a piece of me; maybe a piece of everyone in our town; would simply die. So, I will pledge here tonight, to help in any way I can to save her, because in a strange way she saves a part of me every day. Thank you for allowing me to express my thoughts here tonight folks."

As Stewart Maitland sat down his wife gently put her hand in his and laid her head on his shoulder; tears in her eyes. A visibly touched Mayor Wiggins took back the floor with a big smile on his face and commented.

"Folks, now I know why we are called the Volunteer State." With that comment the whole room laughed out loud while standing and clapping; all seemed to instantly transform into a light hearted mood with hope for the future.

After a few more comments, the Mayor stated.

"Folks, it seems we have come to an agreement to take up a collection of good faith to present to the railway company; let's meet here next week to see what we can come up with as far as an offer."

The Mayor adjourned the meeting for the evening. Ben Bailey left the meeting that night with a full heart of renewed admiration for the Mayor and all of the citizens of Summerville. These were the same people who had shown up to repair his house early one morning after he had come back home to stay. They brought paint, lumber, wallpaper, nails, even refreshments and food. They had repaired his home, but they had done much more than that, they had helped to renew his spirit through their totally unselfish talents, acceptance and kindness. They had repaired his heart. These people were Benjamin Bailey's friends and his new family, and if he could possibly help it, he was not going to let them deplete their life savings without trying something on his own to save the ole No. 2.

As Ben, Paul and Walton Griffin, got far away from the dispersing crowd for a quick private meeting, each knew what the other was thinking.

"Would you two gentlemen agree that maybe it is time to contact Mr. Mark Corrigan?" Ben asked.

"I couldn't agree more." Paul answered.

"You took the words out of my mouth." Walton added.

The three agreed to meet several times before the next town meeting.

A Prayer Answered

The next meeting came quickly with the crowd even larger than before. Mayor Wiggins called the meeting to order and ask for everyone's attention while holding up a mystery letter so everyone could see.

"Ladies and Gentlemen, just last night I received this letter placed on my front door, and to tell you the truth I do not know what to make of it, so, I figured the best thing to do is to just read it to you tonight."

The Mayor carefully pulled the letter out of the envelope, adjusted his tiny wire rimmed glasses and began to read it to the silent and curious crowd.

["*To the good and faithful people of Summerville. It has come to our organization's attention of the dilemma that Railway service through Summerville will be closing soon. We have received all of the facts and want to assure the good citizens you now have nothing to be concerned about as we would like to purchase the railway company in your name. Your brave and individual selfless acts to save the railway have been noted and appreciated, and we will require no funds from you to complete this transaction. However, there are two stipulations to this transaction. The first is, that we turn the management and ownership of the railway over to the citizens of Summerville therefore securing its operations for many years to come; and the second is for you all to accept this proposal with no questions asked of the identity of the purchasers. We hope you will accept this gift from us and we wish the great citizens of Summerville; God's Speed."]*

Mayor Wiggins took the letter and carefully folded it and placed it back into the envelope as if it were made of breakable material. He took off his small round glasses and looked out over a confused and stunned audience, that was so quiet one could only hear the katydids in the trees through the open windows. Benjamin Bailey was sitting across from Paul and Angela. Ben looked at Angela and gave her a quick wink of a job well done; a wink that was quickly returned.The Mayor then said. "Folks I have no answers to any questions as this is just as mysterious to me as it is to you. All I can say is it looks like our prayers have been answered and we will just have to wait and see about this. I will keep you informed of any new developments; I guess well, I guess this meeting is adjourned."

Ben, Paul, Walton and Angela left the meeting with big smiles on their faces. Ben stopped them all when they reached a private area.

"You guys did a great job putting this solution together; I am really grateful." Ben said. There was a moment of silence then Cousin Walton spoke.

"You know, if you guys ever had any doubt of why you found that treasure; I think tonight should put it to rest. It just saved our town." He stated.

"All I can say to that, Brother Walton, is "AMEN." Ben replied.

With that revelation they all headed home for the night. As the ten o'clock run of the No.2 Engine passed through town that night, blowing her proud whistle to signal the final nightly run, the people of Summerville would pause and listen with a new appreciation for the old train, and retire for the night offering a special prayer of thanksgiving; especially, Mr. Stewart Maitland.

The Breakfast Meeting

Time seemed to be passing a little slower in Summerville but Paul was noticing some gray hairs sneaking in between his normally black crown. It was a Saturday morning in early May. Paul and Christopher had finished the early morning chores and were getting ready to join the whole family for a hearty breakfast. The Taylor children were growing up quickly now and seemed to be changing every day. Christopher was now about six foot two and was a strapping young lad as they say. Arielle and Alyssa had grown into the most beautiful young ladies in the state. While washing up Paul noticed Ben's old truck coming up the driveway. He was always amazed how Ben kept this thirty-year-old antique running as well as he did, but the old truck always started and performed to his satisfaction. Paul went out on the porch to meet Ben and invited him to eat breakfast with them.

"It looks like I timed this visit just right; I cannot refuse one of Angela's delicious meals anytime. I'm also glad the whole tribe is here also because I would like to discuss some things with you and the kids." Ben stated.

There was always one thing Paul could count on with Ben and that was one never knew what he was planning at any given time; he had no problem staying busy. After the hearty breakfast and several cups of coffee, Ben ask if all of the children would stay for a few minutes as he wanted to run an interesting idea by all of them.

"So what's on that fertile mind of yours Ben?" Paul inquired.

Ben chuckled and sipped another drink of coffee leaned back in his chair to explain.

"Paul and Angela, I know you probably remember me mentioning a few years ago at our first meeting how I had another couple of things in mind that I wanted to use some of our funds for."

Paul and Angela nodded their heads in agreement with Christopher, Arielle and Alyssa listening in while they finished eating.

"Well I have two projects that I want to do and I want to get your opinions on them." Ben said. "The first has to do with your little ones here at the table, which aren't so little any more. It's hard to believe your beautiful daughters here will graduating before you know it from high school and Chris here stands over six foot; but don't let me get off of the subject or I will be eating lunch with you also." Ben chuckled. The whole family laughed as even the kids were becoming more curious as to what Ben was planning for them.

"Now Paul and Angie, first of all, I don't want any argument from you two on what I am going to say; OK, because it's not going to do you any good as I have already made arrangements to help pay for your kids college education thanks to my good friend and excellent lawyer; Walton Griffin." Ben stated quickly.

Paul and Angela were stunned speechless for a few seconds shaking their heads slowly each hesitating to see which one of them was going to comment first to Ben's announcement. As it happened Paul spoke out first.

"Ben we can't accept something like that; that's a lot of money." Paul answered. "I agree with Paul, Ben, it's too kind of you, but that money is for the people who are in desperation in our town." Angela added.

"Now I understand what you're saying, but just hear me out and humor an old man here." Ben answered."The way I figure it, if Paul and Chris had just given up on the treasure hunt when things got rough out there, there would not be any money today and I still feel bad about Paul not being able to crow a little about his discovery; you know, to the magazines and media. This was Paul's one big break to be in the history books, not to mention those interesting treasure magazines. He gave that up to protect me and this town. Now hear me out you two; neither of you have ever asked me for anything since I met you, and I want to do something for your family. Now, I happen to know that Arielle wants to go into medicine and Alyssa is fancying law school; two noble professions; and Chris here wants to continue his education in the agriculture field and has been working two jobs besides helping on the farm saving for college and I'm here to say that I admire all three of them for their work ethic and that is a tribute to their parents raising them up right. Now, college is expensive and I would be honored if you would let me do this." Ben exclaimed in a stern manner not taking a breath. Paul and Angela gazed at each other in amazement while shaking their heads.

"But Ben, this is too much we can't accept this."

Ben set his coffee cup down and leaned back in his chair interrupting as though he hadn't heard a reply.

"So there, it's settled, now I have another important matter I need your opinion on."

Paul and Angela were getting a kick out of Ben's hardheaded character and chuckling with him as he continued.

"Ben, I think you're the one who should have been the lawyer. You have been hanging around Cousin Walton too long." Paul exclaimed.

"Well, I told you he is one of my favorite people." Ben answered with a chuckle.

Paul and Angela could not wait to hear what idea he was going to present them with next. Ben started to explain his next brainstorm with extra energy and a sparkle in his eye Paul and Angela had not seen since the very first secret Christmas club meeting.

"Both of you know how big my place is; well I've been doing a lot thinking and soul searching lately on how I can turn the old place into something that will do some good and maybe help some other people." Ben said.

"What other people are you referring to Ben?" Paul inquired.

Ben waited as Angela finished pouring him another cup of coffee to explain."I'm talking about our veterans." Ben answered."Paul when your father and I returned from Europe I can still remember the way we felt after we arrived home. Neither of us wanted to talk about our experience or remember certain things mainly because nobody that hadn't experienced what we went through could possibly understand; thank the Good Lord we had each other to talk to. It's the same today all wars are the basically the same except many of the boys coming home have no one they can talk to that under-stands. That being said I was thinking of turning my place into kind of a transition home til some of our vet-erans could get back on their feet. Now I'm not talking about sitting around the fireplace feeling sorry for your-self. I'm talking about putting them to work to help forget. I have over three hundred acres of land that I can find something for these guys to do. Paul you know as well as I do you never run out of work to do on a farm and keeping them busy with hard work can do nothing but help them physically and more important, mentally." Ben stated taking another gulp of coffee." "So far what do you think?" Ben asked.

"Ben, I think that is an outstanding idea." Paul exclaimed.

"I do too Ben; I would be glad to help you decorate the extra rooms." Angela added.

"You have no idea how good that makes me feel; sometimes I wonder about how sane some of my ideas are." Ben exclaimed.

"Well just let us know when you want us to start helping." Paul added.

The rest of the morning the family passed ideas among themselves on how to start the transition home. It was destined to be a great success in the coming years.

The Best Of The Best

efore everyone left the breakfast table that morning Christopher said he needed to talk to the whole family together.

"I guess this is as good of a time as any, especially since I wanted to tell Mr. Ben also. I just wanted to let everyone know that I have been thinking about this for a while now and I have made up my mind on something." Christopher stated.

Everyone was at full attention as this was not part of Christopher's character; he was more of a thinker than a big talker.

"I have decided to join the Marine Corps." He announced.

For a few seconds not a word was spoken at the table. Ben was determined to let Paul and Angela or one of the immediate family respond first. Paul and Angela's face turned into a look that one was not able to read. Ben could not tell if they were happy or sad or just plain surprised. He did know they would be worried about their only son in harm's way for so long. Paul was the first to respond after gaining his composure.

"Christopher, I think your mother and I know you pretty well and you have probably weighed out your decision as best as you can. Just from listening to soldiers and veterans myself I know that it takes a special person to do this job and although we will all be concerned about your safety; you're a grown man now and this is your decision and I support you one hundred per cent; if you are certain that this is what you want to do." Paul said.

Angela was not as certain. Tears had welled up in her eyes but she did not want to appear that she was against her son's plans.

"Maybe you can give me a little while for this to sink in." She said.

Of course Arielle and Alyssa were pelting Christopher with all kinds of questions on what, when, and where he was going. As for Benjamin Bailey he still kept unusually quiet as memories on his own Chris were suddenly revisiting him.

A few days later Christopher felt he needed to visit Ben just to talk. As he entered the gate at the end of the walk, his memories transported him back to the first time he had walked this same path; a petrified ten year old. He thought about the first time he had met Benjamin Bailey; the man he did not realized had saved him from a rattler sinking its one-inch fangs into his juggler that would have surely killed him. Christopher knocked on the door and was met by Ben.

"Well Chris, this is a pleasant surprise although I have to admit I was expecting you to come by before you left for basic." Ben said.

Christopher put his hand out to meet Ben's all the while remembering the first time he had met and shook his hand as a scared little boy looking up into his scary piercing blue eyes. Now Christopher was eye level with Ben and he was noticing how Ben's age was starting to show on him. But the old image of him would be the one Christopher would carry with him the rest if his life.

"Yes Sir, I just wanted to talk to you alone Mr. Ben and see how you are doing. I thought maybe you might give me some words of wisdom about joining up." Christopher replied.

Ben invited Christopher to sit with him on the porch. After they became settled, Ben replied to Christopher.

Ben said. "I just can't believe you are now a grown man; time goes by fast. As for joining the Marines, son, you couldn't be in a better group of men and I understand without you saying another word why you did it; it's because you are a special man and you love your country and you have that inner need to give something back to her. I knew that the first time I met you right here on this spot and have known it ever since. I only have one disappointment about this and that is your Grandfather did not get to see it."

Christopher noticed a crack in Ben's voice.

"I sure do miss your Grandfather." He said.

"I do to Mr. Ben." Christopher replied.

There was a pause as Ben regained his composer.

"Chris, you just remember to be careful and come back home safely; Oh and before I forget it; you just let me know if you or the guys in your unit need anything; remember that treasure you found is not just for the people here in our town; we can share it with your soon to be new colleges. And your mother and I will keep those chocolate chip care baskets coming your way." Ben laughed.

Christopher started to laugh along with Ben and they had more conversation that day. Before Christopher left his house, Ben asked if it was ok if they could say their goodbyes then instead of Ben coming to the train station. Ben became very solemn, and then spoke.

"Chris, I'm just not good at goodbyes like this one, so, I would like to wish you well now and let your family have some private time with you that day; I hope you understand and I have to say I will be praying God protects you every day: I'm really going to miss you son." Ben said with a slight tremble in his voice. "Mr. Ben, that's alright, I do understand more than you know Sir." Christopher replied.

Christopher knew in his heart it was because of Ben's memories of his own Chris haunting him, that he would not be there except in spirit to see him off that day. After about an hour of visiting, Christopher had to leave, so the two parted. As Christopher approached the fence at the end of the lane he turned to wave goodbye one last time before he left for the service. Ben raised his long lanky arm and shouted; "Remember Son, Semper Fi."

Christopher raised his hand in response, "Semper Fi Sir."

Christopher left for basic training a week later on the same train his Grandfather, Benjamin Bailey and thirteen others had boarded so long ago to enter the United States Marine Corps'. Most of the town was there to see him off with well wishes, tears and promises to pray for his safety every day.

Even after the train was completely out of sight from the station and the towns folks had dispersed; the Taylor family still stood on the loading dock, silently, hand in hand until the train whistle faded into the mountains and could be heard no more. They never notice Benjamin Bailey hidden in the shadows, hat in hand with tears streaming down his aging weathered cheeks.

A Worthy Project

The work on the veteran's home started immediately.
Angela and Paul were glad to help Ben on his new
project. They noticed that he seemed to be in more of
a hurry to complete the renovation than usual. Angela
did not mind, as it was one more thing to help keep her
mind off of her only son being in harm's way. Every letter
she would receive from Christopher would be read over
and over again. She noticed she was relying more on
Paul to comfort her with any words of encouragement.
She didn't realize how much Paul was also relying on
her for the same. One day while the three were hard at
work finishing up some minor details, Ben approached
them asking for their opinion.

"I have been giving it a lot of thought on what we can name this place when we are finished. I just don't like the words halfway house for a name; it sounds like somebody is sleeping off a bad drunk." Ben said.

Paul and Angela could not help but laugh, mostly because they agreed with Ben's opinion.

"I think we should think up something completely different." Paul replied. Ben rubbed his chin deep in thought.

"I agree. What about this?" "THE VETERANS RANCH." Ben replied.

Angela spoke up with an idea. "What about, THE BENJAMIN BAILEY VETERANS RANCH." She said. Paul interjected. "Yeah Angie, I like it that has a good ring to it."

Ben kept rubbing his chin and slowly shook his head. "I don't know about that, that might sound a bit too uppity. I'm trying to keep a low profile in this you know." Ben answered.

I don't think anyone in this town will think you are uppity Ben; they know what kind of friend and man you are." Paul replied. "I agree two hundred per cent Ben." Angela said.

Ben took a few seconds to answer. "Well, let me just mull it over in my head and think about it; but I appreciate the kind words from you two anyway."

It did not take long to get Ben's home presentable for the future tenants. The old mansion was furnished to accommodate around twenty people very comfortably. Many of the ladies of the town volunteered to cook and help clean when needed. Bobi Stone had framed a military picture of James Bennett Taylor, which was hung next to Christopher Bailey's in the drawing room. Ben strategically placed a light above both of the pictures that was to never be turned off. The room was to serve as a gathering place for the soldiers just to relax and talk. Pastor Robert Major would come over once a week to hold a Bible meeting or counseling if needed. Pastor Major helped Ben anyway he could and was a virtual jack of all trades especially when it came to renovations. He had become one of Ben's favorite people in the town. It looked like everything was set to host the new part time tenants. Now all that had to be done was get the word around. Ben's only fear was that too many would show up at once but his fears were unfounded. In the next few month's a few veterans started to trickle in. There were even a few guys from Christopher's outfit that came. They would stay for a while work on the ranch just to help clear their minds and souls of war then one day they would decide it was time to return to society and resume their lives. Every one of them would carry a piece of the home and the kindness of the town's people back to their own homes. Many would return years later just to visit and sometimes volunteer to help. Ben made many new friends in the time he ran the home and it was viewed as a great success. It created a unexplainable satisfying feeling in Ben's heart.

Misty

*W*hen Christopher Taylor was in the sixth grade his teacher introduced Misty Montgomery to the class. She was a new student that moved to Summerville from just a county over. Misty's grandmother had a farm and was in need of help to run it so her parents moved in to assist her. Christopher was instantly smitten with Misty and unknowingly to him despite both of their shyness, she was just as interested in him. The two became good friends with Christopher even letting her in the tree house, to Monte and Sam's objection, where supposedly no girls were ever to be allowed.

One day Misty did not come to school, which was not like her as she was one who loved school and was a straight A student. That day the teacher asks for everyone's attention and relayed the news that Misty's mother was very ill. Although she gave no details on her illness everyone could tell it was serious as she was almost in tears just informing the class. About a week later the bad news came that Misty's mother had died. It was that day that Christopher went to Ben Bailey and told him what had happened. Ben told Christopher not to worry he would look into it and see what was going on.

After her mother's death Misty's father was unable to cope with his sadness and the farm was not doing well. This topped off with the weather not cooperating for the crops and the expenses of equipment repair were putting them in a very bad way. The town's folks helped all they could but it seemed like a double lost cause. Misty's father fell far behind on his land payments. He would try to hide bad things from her whenever he could but one night before she went to bed she passed by her father's room and heard his voice through the cracked door. Her father was down on his knees by his bed praying for help. He had received a call to be at a meeting at the bank the next day to discuss some important business. He knew they were going to take the farm. He did not even notice his only daughter entering the room until she bowed down beside him and slipped her thin little fingers in his hand. They both prayed for Gods help and cried together.

The next day Misty's father made the meeting with the banker. The banker had a stern business look on his face and asked if he would follow him into his private office. Misty's nervous father sat down in the plush leather chair across the desk from the bank official. The Banker reached in the right drawer and pulled out an envelope and handed it to Misty's dad.

"I think you know why we are here Mr. Montgomery." He said.

"Yes, I believe I do." He answered.

"Well, before you come to any conclusions I suggest you open that envelope and read the contents very carefully." The Banker instructed.

Misty's father reluctantly opened the letter and slowly read the contents silently. A slow smile began to take over his face. The letter said his back payments and the coming year's payment were paid in full. Misty's father looked at the banker in unbelief. "I don't think I understand this." He said.

The Banker leaned back in his high back chair and smiled. "That makes two of us Mr. Montgomery; all I can tell you is I received your debt payment in the mail with instructions to contact you and give you this letter in person that you are now holding in your hands. Your debt has been paid in full." He finished.

Misty's father drove home in a numbed state thanking God all the way home. He informed Misty and her grandmother of what had transpired and in the coming years would pull the letter out just to read it one more time. He called it his miracle letter. It would be several years later that Misty would find out just who were the ones responsible for helping restore hers and her father's faith.

After high school graduation Christopher and Misty lost touch with each other as she was accepted into a college that was across the country and she rarely could come home to visit. Although Christopher would never see her, he would think about her often and she always claimed a special place in his heart.

A Passed Tragedy

As Paul grew older, he was beginning to see the image of his father as he would look into the mirror. That would often trigger a bitter sweet memory that had changed his life forever.

When Paul was sixteen years old he had become a lover of any kind of sport, especially the outdoor kind. He was a talented football player for his high school team. His outstanding asset was his speed. He was also the fastest runner on his track team in the county and was well on his way to a great future in every sport he participated in. It was just a matter of which one he wanted to pursue. Paul had started planning his life and had decided to keep the family tradition of joining the Marines after graduating and then attend college after being discharged. His life's plan was nothing that was suggested by his father or mother, friends or classmates; it was just something that seemed to be inborn in him since he could remember. It was on his mind every single day and had become a private obsession. He could hardly wait to serve his country just as his father and grandfather before him.

Paul also loved horses and had become an accomplished horseman. He mostly just rode for fun, as horseback riding came in handy on the ranch where it was practically a necessity.

One morning Paul's father asked him to check on the herd at the back of the ranch. His father also reminded him to be sure to dismount and lead his horse around a particular dangerous location that required passing around a deep ravine on a ledge about five feet wide at the widest point. This was a path Paul had taken probably a hundred times before with his father, however this time he decided to ride his horse across the ledge instead of dismounting and leading him over safely as he had been instructed by his father. Paul was riding his horse that he was given on his eighth birthday. He had named him Flash, as he was the fastest quarter horse the town had ever seen and had earned Paul countless ribbons in the local horse shows.

About half way across the ravine a raccoon darted in front of him coming out of nowhere, and spooked Flash. Flash suddenly bolted backward with his back legs loosing footing in the loose dirt at the edge of the cliff. Paul managed to stay in the saddle but the unstable dirt gave way and the two plummeted backward ultimately landing half way down the steep hill with their fall being broken only by the small boulders and sharp saplings and stumps. For some reason Paul hung on and did not fall off. When finally reaching the stopping point of the fall, Paul's right leg was totally crushed along with his pelvis; there was a gaping wound on the side of his right leg and he was trapped under Flash who had broken two of his legs in the fall. To make the situation even worse Flash would try to get to his feet from time to time further grinding Paul's leg between the saddle and the rocky earth. The pain was almost unbearable and Paul felt himself slipping into unconsciousness. He managed to reach his rifle and through tears of fear and pain, shot Flash to keep him from moving. In one last desperate act, he then unloaded his rifle in repetitive shots until it was empty praying someone would hear them and come to the rescue. Paul thought his life was over.

Paul's father was at the house feeding the livestock when he heard the unusual volley of rifle shots. He found his son about a half hour later. Not having the time to get help somehow Paul's father managed to lift Flash off of his son's crushed and bleeding leg. Fearing that putting Paul across his saddle might worsen his condition; he carried his son in his arms all of the way back to the house. The last thing Paul would remember before slipping into unconsciousness would be feeling his father's heart pounding through the thick leather jacket as he carried his son home.

Paul stayed in the county hospital for many days and when he finally was able to come home he had gone into a miserable depression of guilt and sadness over having to shoot the horse he loved and a deep remorse for the result of his disobedience. To try to ease his constant guilt, Paul had secretly decided he would never mount another horse as long as he lived. When he had healed just enough, his father, seeing his son's despair, rose extra early one Saturday morning, saddled two horses and made a reluctant Paul mount up again. The two had a mostly silent ride until they ultimately ended up at the ravine where the accident occurred.

JB Taylor could see the fear on his son's face but Paul did not protest; he then helped his son dismount and they led the two horses across the ravine. Upon reaching the back half of ranch with their horses at a slow walk Paul's father broke his silence and began to talk to his son.

"Son, when I was about a year older than you are now I had something very tragic happen to me that I still think about sometimes to this very day, and will never forget for the rest of my life; but that's because it served to change my life."

Paul was all ears as he sensed something different about his Father today; he had never seen him in a mood like this. His father continued the story.

"I had a friend named Tom Martin; we had been friends for a long time I guess you could say we grew up together. One hot day right after the spring thaw we decided to go swimming in the creek. We had not been swimming since winter ended and we just thought we couldn't wait any longer. My father had warned me more than once to never go swimming in that creek when the water was high because of, what we called "whirlpools" in my day. The water would be so high and forceful it would create whirlpool swirls that if you got sucked into one it was almost impossible to swim out and it would hold you under until you drowned. Well, Tom and I went anyway; he jumped in first and got caught in one of those whirlpools. I tried everything I knew how to do and almost drowned myself, but I was unable to save him. The image of him trying to grasp my hand and ultimately disappearing under the current will haunt me forever as I was powerless to save him. I had never felt so miserable and low in all of my life; even though Tom's family never blamed me; it didn't help; nothing helped. I didn't think anything could ever help me with my guilt. It was eating me alive."

Paul was unable to say any words to his father and just listened. His Father continued.

"My father noticed the change in me and was concerned in his own way."

Paul's father stopped his horse. Paul followed his lead.

"You never knew your Grandfather but he would have gotten a kick out of you. He was a serious man; stern with us, but always fair, he wasn't one to ever express love verbally but he had a way of letting you know he loved you although sometimes you didn't realize it until years later; I am still amazed at some of my memories that pop back into my head from time to time that make me aware of just why he did things the way he did." James said.

"One day we were out in the field way behind on the harvest because of the rain; my father parked the mule then came up to me and said;"James I want to talk to you about something."

"I had just received a draft notice and was going to go to war soon so I assumed he was going to tell me some things to watch out for as he himself had been to war years before. We went over to a large shade tree at the end of the field and sat down. Leaning against that old tree I started to eat my lunch. I thought it strange that he didn't touch his lunch the whole day and seemed nervous in a strange sort of way. He waited a few minutes and started to talk; not at all about the army, but more about Tom Martin's drowning."

"He said to me."

"James, I know you're feeling real bad about Tom and I just want to tell you it ain't your fault son; now

I don't know a lot of things but I do know you and if you could have saved Tom you would have done it; your Ma and me are worried cause, right now, you don't need to be worrying about this bad thing that happened especially when your over across that ocean just trying to stay alive. Son, you didn't know this; but yesterday Tom's Ma and Pa came over to see me and wanted to see you but you weren't here; they just wanted to tell you thank you for trying to save Tom's life and they knew how sad you are bout it and they are praying for you."

"My father paused after that and seemed to try to choose his words more carefully, probably trying not to preach to me or seem like he was lecturing or angry. He then took out his red handkerchief and wiped his brow and continued." James said.

"James, the Martin's are good people and the way I see it if they aren't blaming you for this tragedy maybe you should quit blaming yourself, son. Besides frettin is a sin and it will eat you up if you let it. Now, I'm going back to work; but I want you to stay here under this tree for as long as you need; till you decide to make peace with this, with yourself, and the Good Lord." Paul's father continued his story.

"Then my father quickly stood up, brushed off the backside of his worn out overalls and walked a few steps back toward the plow mules. Then, he stopped, turned around and said in a cracked, urgent voice."

"James, just know this, your Ma and I love you son."

"He then turned around and went back to work and it was never mentioned again." James Taylor then paused with his story; and addressed his own son.

"Paul, I will never forget that day as long as I live; that was the first time my father had said in words that he loved me. Well sir, I took his advice; I did make my peace with myself and with the Lord. I felt like someone had lifted a heavy boulder off of my back but more important than that, I had no more guilt feelings in my heart and I learned guilt can destroy your soul if you let it. A few weeks later I left for the war."

James continued. "After I got settled in boot camp right before I was shipped overseas, I found some time to write my father a letter to tell him how much he meant to me and thanked him for our talk, or maybe I should say, his talk, and how I was proud to carry his name and that I loved him."

Paul's father paused, took a deep breath, and continued. "My father died a few months after he received my letter and I did not get to say a final good bye to him as I had already left on a ship to go to Europe. Tom Martin's family helped my mother bring in the crop that year.

When I returned home after the war, my mother filled me in on all of the past news and she told me through tear filled eyes that my father got my letter and carried it with him in his coat pocket every place he went, even to the fields. She said she would often observe him through the window as he sat on the front porch at the end of a hard day, and he would pull it out and read it over and over again. She placed it in his coat pocket when she said her final goodbye to him."

Paul and his father had now reached a stopping point at the back of the ranch that overlooked the quiet valley with Paul hanging on every word his dad was speaking. He had never heard this story about his grandfather. James Taylor stopped talking for a moment and gazed at the sight revisiting the past. He then continued.

"You know Son, I wasn't sold much on reading things into life that happen to us every day, I just read the Good Book and do what it says and trust in the Lord; but when my mother told me the day my father died, he had just wanted to take a walk and they found him sitting under the very tree where he gave me my life changing talk; I have to confess, I excused myself from the conversation and went out on the porch and cried my eyes out. It gives me peace to think that maybe, just maybe, the last earthly thing he was thinking about was how much he loved me and how much I loved him. Now, I thank God that I took his advice."

James Bennett Taylor had finished his story. Father and Son turned around to head back to the house. On the slow ride back, James Taylor finished his personal mission to help his son.

"Son, sorry for being so long winded, but I think by telling you this, what I am trying to say to you is; yes you have gone through a lot in the past year, but things do happen for a reason whether they be good or bad; it rains on the just and unjust. What you have to do now to survive emotionally is realize your life is not over by a long shot, and disappointments are still going to assault you; some will be small and some may be even larger than the one you are struggling with now, but it is part of growing up and being the man God wants you to be. You and I both made mistakes by disobeying our parents and we have paid for it immensely; now we have to move forward and discover our other hidden talents and plan for our lives that God is trying to reveal to us."

James Bennett Taylor looked across to Paul who was silently taking in everything his dad was saying.

"Son, do you understand what I am saying?" He asked.

Paul shook his head and answered. "Yes Dad, I do."As the two reached the house, Paul's father realized his son's leg might be stiff from the long ride and started to help him down from his mount.

"Dad." Paul said. James Taylor paused from his task.

"Yes Son." James answered.

"Can I try to do this myself just to see if I can?" Paul asked.

James paused for a moment and then replied."Son those words are music to my ears; go ahead I'm here if you need me."

"I know Dad, you always have been." Paul replied.

Paul secured both feet solidly on the ground with little trouble.

"Here, I will help you unsaddle these fine animals." Paul's Father said.

"That's ok Dad, you go ahead and take a break; I would like to do this myself; I need to get back into practice and I have some thinking to do; and Dad.

Paul looked at his father through tearful eyes; "Thanks."

Paul's father sported a big smile. "Son, you are going to be just fine; oh, and by the way, I noticed Brent Whitaker has a horse he wants to sell; he reminds me a lot of Flash, maybe we can go look at him tomorrow."

Paul nodded his head in agreement. "That would be great Dad."

Paul's father told him to come in as soon as he finished as his mother had prepared an extra special lunch for them. After he took a few steps toward the house his father stopped, made a half turn and spoke. "Remember Son, your mother and I love you."

Paul paused just trying to hold back the tears. "I love you too Dad." He replied.

As Paul's father walked toward the house, Paul paused from unhitching the saddle girt on his horse just to watch the six foot four figure of his father reach his destination, while still absorbing his personal experience that he had revealed to him.

It would be a few years later as Paul grew into manhood, that his limp would disappear completely and most of the emotional scars would fade; however, It would still be many more years before his disappointment of missing out on his dream of military service would heal. From time to time a slight twinge of pain would revisit Paul in his injured leg, but instead of complaining, Paul would silently offer up a prayer of thanks and would use it as a fond reminder of the day he took that life-changing ride with his father.

That day Paul no longer looked upon his father just as a protector and provider. That day, Paul's father became his hero.

A Present Tragedy

It was a nippy fall Saturday morning and Paul's cattle herd had started calving. For some reason it was never understood by any farmer or rancher why there was always one cow that would disappear and try to hide in harm's way to have her newborn as far away from the safe warm barn as she could get. This particular morning Paul came up one short on his daily count. He gobbled down an early breakfast and saddled his horse. Horseback was by far the most thorough way to search for a headstrong mamma cow. Paul made sure to carry a strong rope and his rifle. Many times he had spoiled an easy meal for hungry coyotes by arriving just in time before they would kill the newborn calf. This day he was having trouble finding the cow and had burned a half a day looking but today he didn't mind as he was able to enjoy the beauty of the changing foliage and watch as the sunrise seemed to set afire the beautiful maples, oaks and sycamores that seemed to be in a contest to outdo the other with their breathtaking colors. The unmistakable aroma of freshly cut hay filled the air as the sun rays burned off the morning dew in the valley to awaken another magnificent day.

Finally, Paul found the mother cleaning up her newborn bull calf. Paul draped the calf over his saddle to the mother's objections and proceeded to carry it back to the barn with the mother bellowing all the way back with her protest. When he arrived home Angela met him with a concerned look on her face.

"Paul, something has happened to Ben; he was taken to the county hospital this morning." Angela said.

"Do you know any details?" Paul quizzed.

Angela was helping Paul unsaddle the horse as she was speaking.

"They believe he had a heart attack." She answered.

Paul secured the mother and calf in a stall and walked quickly back to the house with Angela.

"I'm going to get cleaned up and go see what is going on; do you want to come with me Angie?"

"Yes, I do." Angela answered. "I will tell the kids where we are going and I will be ready when you are."

When they arrived at the hospital Ben Bailey was already secured in a room and was asleep. The Doctors met them and gave them some details of what they knew about the seriousness of Ben's condition. Paul and Angela were so distressed that they did not recognize who one of the Doctor's was; however, she did recognize them but realized how upset they were with Ben's condition. She also realized they had not seen her since she was in High School. She decided if she had the opportunity later on maybe she could socialize with them on the latest in Summerville, but for now she was also concerned about Ben's condition and was working very closely with the other Doctors to try and save his life.

Paul had found out that day Ben had stopped to help a man with a flat tire. When he passed out the farmer brought him to the hospital. For the next few hours and coming days Paul and Angela would take turns sitting with Ben. He was very weak and could speak but only with a soft voice. Paul had tried to relay a message to Christopher of the situation but had no way of knowing if he received the news or not. On the third day of his hospital stay Paul and Angela were both there to sit with him. Ben seemed to be asleep but suddenly opened his eyes and put a big smile on his face. He was staring passed the two toward the doorway. Paul and Angela turned to see what he was smiling at. There in the doorway was Christopher Taylor in his Marine uniform. He had managed to get a leave. Paul and Angela immediately hurried over to hug their son. Christopher gave them both the biggest and longest hug he had could produce. Paul and Angela could not hold back their tears, as could Christopher. After more hugs and tears Christopher softly asked how Mr. Ben was doing.

"I'd say your probably better medicine than anything they have here Son." Paul answered.

"You go sit with him and we will give you some privacy." Angela said.Christopher approached Ben's bed and stood beside him. Ben was still smiling as Christopher took his feeble hand.

"Your about the best looking Marine I have seen in a while Chris." Ben said in a weak voice.

Christopher pulled up a chair and sat down beside the bed.

"It is so good to see you son; I've been praying for your safety every day. "Ben whispered.

"It is good to see you too Sir, how are you feeling?" Christopher asked.

"Oh, I'll be fine son, you know they gave me the prettiest Doctor you have ever seen and she and the Nurses are taking good care of this old man. I would like for you to meet them, do you think you could sit with me a while?" Ben asked.

Christopher put his hat on the small table near the bed. "I would be honored Sir, we have a lot of catching up to do." Christopher answered.

Ben seemed to be getting his spirits back and was enjoying talking with Christopher. When the visit was around forty-five minutes old, the Doctor and Nurse came in to administer Ben's medicine and complete their nightly check. Ben acknowledged her when she entered the room.

"I thought you had forgotten about me." He said joking. "I want you to meet someone."

As the Doctor approached the bed in the dimly lit room her face came into the light. As Christopher rose to formally meet her he couldn't believe his eyes.

"Misty, Is that you?'

"Hello Chris, yes it's me, it's been too long since I saw you last."

Without hesitation Christopher walked around the end of the hospital bed with Misty meeting him half way. She put her arms around the waste of the six foot two Marine and gave him a tight hug which was willingly returned by Christopher. Now Ben Bailey had an even bigger smile on his face as the two made small talk catching up on old times. His plan had worked.

"Why don't you two go get some coffee and do some more catching up on what you have been up to all these years, you've got all night to stick me with these needles?" Ben exclaimed.

"That sounds like a good idea Mr. Ben; I haven't seen Misty for a very long time." Christopher answered.

Misty finished her duties while talking to Christopher and gave Ben his nightly medicine. He slowly started to drift off to sleep. Christopher and Misty said good night to Ben and left his room.

Old Times

Christopher and Misty went out into the hospital hallway.

"Misty it is so good to see you we have got to spend some time together while I'm on leave." Christopher exclaimed.

"I would like that very much." Misty declared. "My shift is over now, so I'm game." Christopher hesitated suddenly remembering he had not even been home yet to talk to his parents. He had come straight to the hospital from the train station.

"I've got a great idea, come home and eat supper with us. I know my parents would like to see you again and they are in the waiting room now. "Christopher said.

"I think that would be nice; I saw them yesterday but did not get a chance to even say hello; I just got back into town myself just a few days ago. Are you sure I won't be imposing coming unannounced?" She inquired.

Christopher laughed. "Are you kidding they would love to see you and catch up. It will make their day to see you again, you were always their favorite."

Christopher suddenly felt a new energy that helped temporarily forget his concern of seeing a very frail Ben Bailey in that hospital bed. Paul and Angela were waiting for Christopher in the waiting room and were very happy to see Misty.

"I still don't see how we missed you." Angela remarked.

After the hugs and welcome homes Angela suggested that Misty come and join them for supper.

"See Misty, I didn't even have to ask her, she beat me to the punch." Christopher said.

Angela and Paul noticed how happy Christopher seemed to be running into Misty and likewise on Misty's part. They all sat down to supper after about an hour and talked about many things that had happened since Misty had left town for college and Medical school.

"So Misty, your actually on the verge of being a full fledge Cardiologist; is that correct?" Paul asked.

"Yes Sir, I have been going to school seems like my whole life now just trying to finish and practice, hopefully it won't be long now. Mr. Bailey is one of my first patient's and likes to kid with me. He is a very nice man., but he is very sick. He really needs much rest his heart is very weak. "She answered.

"He has done a lot for this town and the people in it; one day when you have more time maybe I can tell you about him." Paul said.

"I would like that Mr. Taylor; I would like that very much. We also need to pray for him." Misty said.

They all agreed and finished up the meal. Christopher and Misty walked out on the front porch to talk.

"She is a special girl Paul." Angela commented.

"Yes she is, and I detected some special feelings going on between them." Paul added. "So did I." Angela agreed.

"Christopher has liked Misty since they were three feet tall, but now I think it is a little more than like; I think he is in love with her." Paul added.

"So you caught the looks he had when she was talking too." Angela answered.

"How could you miss them, they were obvious even to me." Paul said.

The both laughed and finished the dishes.

The Front Porch

Christopher and Misty went out on the front porch and sat down on the porch swing. It was a beautiful clear fall night with a full moon. The two talked and laughed about high school days and what had become of some of their classmates. Even though it had been a few years, Misty felt very close to Christopher. It was like they were still in school. It was obvious to her now that she was really in love with him and the years apart had not diminished her feelings for him in the slightest, they just sealed them in her heart.

"Chris, can I ask you a somewhat personal question?" She asked.

"Sure Misty." A somewhat apprehensive Christopher answered.

"Why did you not ask me out while we were in high school?" Misty quizzed. Christopher's face turned a beet red that was even evident in the pale moonlight. He then started to rub is forehead not noticing Misty biting her lip trying not to laugh at his reaction.

"Well, I guess you could say I was scared you would say no and that would have just crushed my ego." He answered, with tongue in cheek trying not to laugh.

"After all, you were the prettiest girl I had ever laid eyes on." He replied.

"OK, I guess that's a good enough answer." Misty giggled.

"Well, I'm glad you liked it after all I am a Marine and we never lie." Christopher laughed.

"Now, it's my turn to ask a question." Christopher inquired.

"Well, just go ahead and asked, Mr. Marine." Misty returned still giggling.

Christopher leaned back in the swing purposely hesitating with his question.

"If I had asked you out, would you have said yes Doctor Montgomery?"

Both were now enjoying the friendly sparing. "I don't know Mr. Marine, I'll have think about it and call you in the morning." She said laughing out loud.

"Oh, that really hurts Doc. tell you what, let me pick you up tomorrow for lunch and take you to a special place and you can tell me then." Christopher said. "That sounds good; I'll check my calendar and see if I have any other Marines picking me up tomorrow for lunch; oh, I just remembered, I don't." They both laughed.

It was getting late; Christopher took Misty back to the hospital to check on Ben before she retired for the night. Christopher walked her up to the door. Misty turned and gave him a hug and kissed him on the cheek. She looked him in the eyes and said. "For your information Mr. Handsome Marine, the answer to your question would have been yes."

Christopher smiled as his heart melted. He leaned down and kissed Misty.

"I'll pick you up tomorrow Doc." He said.

Misty returned with another kiss. "I'm looking forward to it, Mr. Marine."

A Picnic To Remember

Christopher woke the next morning with a song in his heart looking forward to his date with Misty. When he arrived downstairs for breakfast Paul and Angela were already there finishing their morning coffee.

"We thought you might sleep a little late today." Paul said.

"No, in fact I was up half the night just doing some thinking about things." Christopher replied.

"Now would that be just things or a special girl." Angela said while winking at Paul.

"What do you think of her?" Christopher asked. Before either Paul or Angela could answer Christopher blurted out. "I think she is great." He said.

"We do too son." Paul replied. "In fact we have something we would like to give to you." Paul reached in his shirt pocket and pulled out a box and gave it to Christopher.

"What is this Dad?" He asked.

"Open it." Paul instructed.

As Christopher opened the little blue felt covered box Paul started to explain. "This was your grandmother's ring which was passed down to her from her mother. Before she passed she told me to give it to you for your future bride."

Angela pulled a handkerchief from her pocket and began to dab her eyes.

Christopher opened the box to find the most beautiful antique diamond ring he had ever seen. Christopher was stunned. He paused for a moment.

"How did you know what I was up to today?" He inquired.

"Well Son when you've seen as much as your mother and I have you somehow just know these things." Paul answered.

Angela started to laugh through her tears of joy. "Now Paul, tell him the truth." She said. Angela wiped the last tear from her eyes.

"The fact of the matter is Christopher we could tell you are in love with each other and we would love to have her as part of this family, but only when you both are ready." Angela added.

Christopher looked down at the ring again. "Thanks Dad, Thanks Mom, I know she will love it, it is the most beautiful ring I have ever seen. Now if she will just say yes I can rest easy."

Angela moved over and sat down by her son.

"Sweetheart, I can tell Misty loves you and you love her, don't worry about anything; it will work out for you; just remember we love you and will stand behind you and Misty whatever you two decide to do."

That morning Paul and Angela went to the hospital to sit with Ben. When they came back a very nervous Christopher borrowed the truck to pick up Misty. Angela had prepared them a picnic lunch. Christopher had a special afternoon planned for her. After picking Misty up Christopher told her he was taking her to a special place. Before they arrived he told her to close her eyes until they arrived. After he stopped the truck.

"OK you can open your eyes now." He said anxiously. When Misty opened her eyes she was surprised and delighted to see the old tree house.

"I can't believe it's still here Chris." She said.

"I hope it will always be here and if it's up to my Dad it will be. He comes up here and repairs it every year." He replied. Misty climbed out of the truck and slowly walked up the hill toward the tree house.

"It's just like I remembered. It's still looks the same; I was afraid to even ask you about it thinking maybe it was gone by now." She said.

The two climbed up the wooden latter and enjoying the view and the lunch along with a gentle cool breeze. "You know Misty you hold a standing record with this tree house; you're the only girl who was ever invited to come into it, my sisters would sneak in from time to time but you were invited by me." Christopher said.

"I seem to remember your friends didn't like that much." She replied.

"Well, they got over it." He said with a smile.

"You were always so nice to me when we were younger Chris; I never forgot that; it's perfect being here again. Thank you for bringing me here. I really needed this." Misty said softly. "It's my pleasure." Christopher answered.

There was a moment of silence.

"Chris I probably should apologize to your parents for last night telling them about Mr. Bailey's condition."

"I don't understand, apologize for what?" He replied. Misty looked out over the mountains and valley and paused for a moment. "Don't think I'm silly but after my mother died something happened to me that changed my life forever; something that brought me back to my trust in God."

"What was that Misty?" Christopher inquired.

Misty told Christopher the whole story of what had happened to her and her father with the overdue bank note and the miracle of someone paying their land note and the letter; that wonderful haunting letter with those kind words burned in her heart that she would never forget. As Christopher listened he suddenly remembered how he had told Ben Bailey of her troubles but never heard any else about it since. Misty started reciting what the letter said and Christopher unwittingly out of habit simultaneously finished it with her, word for word. Misty suddenly stopped her story; her mind was now putting together what had just happened.

"Chris, how, how do you know what the letter said?" She asked desperately. "I have never told anyone about it."

An eerie and almost numbed feeling suddenly came over Christopher; why did he just do that? He could not tell if Misty was angry, happy or just surprised. Maybe she felt betrayed by not knowing.

There was a stunning silence as her beautiful emerald green eyes started to fill with tears. He reached out and pulled her to his chest and started to explain. By now Misty was sobbing and was unable to even talk. "Misty, I need to explain something to you and it is a long story; can I explain it to you? I'm sorry you're sad or angry with me." He said.

Misty pulled back slightly from Christopher and wiped her tears. "I'm not angry with you Chris, if anything you have just made me so happy to even know you had anything to do with my experience you probably don't realize that you help save my father's life that day."

Christopher gently pulled Misty close to him and rubbed her hair as she rested her head on his chest. "Misty." He said in a gentle voice.

"Yes." She answered through her intermittent sobs.

"Will you marry me?" He asked.

Misty looked up at Christopher with a surprised look on her face as she wiped away her tears. Before she could answer, a very nervous Christopher started to explain.

"Misty, I sort of had a speech for you but it looks like I kinda ruined it; all I can tell you is I think I have loved you since the day we met, now don't laugh at me; the truth is, even though I never see you I still think about you every day; I wonder what you're doing, how your making out; those kind of thoughts, and when I saw you the other day my heart melted; I was just afraid your last name might not be Montgomery anymore or you were engaged. All I know is how I feel about you and I want to love and take care of you the rest of your life."

Misty's tears of happiness began to flow. She dabbed them with her handkerchief. Without saying a word she stood on her tiptoes and threw her arms around Christopher's neck and kissed him. She then planted her head against his chest and gave him the tightest hug she could muster out of her small frame.

"Christopher Taylor, I would be honored to be your wife as I too have loved you since the first time you brought me to this tree house." She replied.Christopher reached in his pocket and pulled out his Grandmother's ring and gently slipped it on Misty's petite little finger. It was a perfect fit."This was my Grandmother's, now I want you to have it for the rest of your life." He said.

Misty looked down at her hand gently resting inside of Christopher's almost twice the size of hers.

"It's beautiful." She said with a slight trembling in her voice. "I would be honored to be your wife. This is the happiest day of my life." She whispered.

Ben's Legacy

*B*efore they left the tree house, Christopher told Misty the whole story of how Ben had saved his life, the treasure hunt, and the special club Ben and a few more citizens had formed to use the treasure to help the people of Summerville. Misty was fascinated by the story and had many questions. It all was starting to make sense now. It seems it was Ben who was sending her money at school from time to time anonymously. It would always come in her greatest time of need. Ben had become close friends with Misty's father and would keep up with her through general conversations with him from time to time. That is how he knew so much about her and specifically asked for her to take care of him.

"I have no idea of how many people the treasure has helped. There are probably plenty more stories we will never know about unless my Dad tells us about them, but he, like me has honored Ben's wishes. I'm glad you now know the truth about Mr. Ben and what a great man he is." Christopher then started to laugh.

"What is it?" Misty asked.

"It just hit me why Mr. Ben was so anxious that I was to be sure and meet you that day and why he was adamant that I could not leave until I did; even is his weak condition he was matchmaking." Christopher said slowly shaking his head.

Misty gently nodded her head while still holding Christopher's hand.

"We have had some nice conversations even in the short time I have known him. He told me about that special Christmas Eve when he became a Christian and how much he loved you and your family. Now your stories make me realize just how special he is." She said.

The couple talked for a few more minutes then drove back to the hospital.

As time progressed with the months and years passing, even more revelations of Benjamin Bailey's kindness were revealed to Misty. The more she learned about this man the more her love and respect for Benjamin Bailey would grow.

Six months would pass before First Lieutenant Christopher Paul Taylor and Dr. Misty Montgomery would be married. In the years to follow; on every anniversary of their engagement day, Christopher would prepare a lunch and take Misty to the tree house to celebrate the day he asked the love of his life to marry him where they would spend the whole afternoon together. They would keep this tradition for the rest of their lives.

Happiness And Sorrow

Christopher and Misty wasted no time after their afternoon together meeting Paul and Angela back at the hospital. Upon arriving they did not have to say a word as the smiles of happiness glowed on their faces. The couple found Paul and Angela taking a break from sitting with Ben in the waiting room. Christopher could tell his father was concerned about Ben, but he didn't feel like this was the time to inquire on the subject just yet.

"Dad, Mom, we have some great news for you." Christopher said.

Not letting on they already had guessed, Paul and Angela responded.

"What news would that be?" They said in unison.

"Misty and I are getting married." Christopher blurted out.

Paul turned to Misty. "Misty are you sure you want to marry this guy?" He said jokingly.

"Well, I had to think about it for, for, about two seconds but I am sure as I'm standing here." She answered.

"Now Paul, leave them alone." Angela said as she hugged them both. "I am so happy for you two; Paul we are going to have another daughter." She said.

"I already feel like we do." Paul answered as he hugged his future daughter in law. "I can only tell you two if you have just a fraction of the happiness we have had you will have a great life together." Paul said.

Angela looked at Paul and smiled.

After the announcement Misty asked how Ben was doing.

"He looks like he is getting weaker." Paul said.

"I will go keep a close eye on him tonight and keep you updated." Misty replied.

"Maybe some good news will make him feel better; why don't you two go tell him the big news." Paul suggested.

"That's a good idea Dad; come on Misty let's go tell him." Christopher said. The couple entered Ben's room and Christopher tried not to show the shock on his face of just how much weaker Ben looked. As they approached his bed Ben began to smile.

"Well Chris it looks like you made a great decision today and it looks like she said yes by the look on your faces." Ben said.

"Mr. Ben, how did you know I was going to pop the question today?" Christopher quizzed.

"Son I saw the look on your face when you saw my angel of mercy come in that day and there is no mistaking that look; and that goes for you too young lady." He said turning his head to Misty.

"Mr. Ben you are unbelievable." Christopher answered. Misty bent down and gently kissed Ben on his cheek. "Yes, you really are unbelievable in more ways than I can ever know; how can I ever thank you?" She asked with a tears in her eyes.

"Just by taking care of each other and loving each other with unconditional love my dear; and just remember that powerful word "patience." I am so happy for you two." Ben answered.

"Chris, you have found a real treasure here and that's what's important." Ben said.

The couple spent a few more minutes with Ben filling him in on their plans until he drifted off to sleep. Christopher volunteered to stay with him that night while a very tired Misty caught up on her other patient's needs. She would check back with them early in the morning. Misty didn't have to say a word to Christopher, as he could see Ben's condition was becoming worse.

John 14:1

While Christopher was sitting with Ben that night, around 2:30 he suddenly awakened and gently called Christopher's name. Christopher pulled his chair closer to Ben's bed. Ben raised his left hand and Christopher put his hand in Ben's. In a weak voice Ben started to talk to his friend.

"Son my time has come to go home; please tell your mom and dad and sisters how much I love them just as I love you, and take good care of your little Misty, she is truly a rare treasure in this world and she loves you so much. You two bring back wonderful memories of another couple I knew a long time ago."

Ben slowly raised his feeble right hand to his forehead in a trembling salute and held it there until Christopher naturally rose out of his chair. Christopher knew this was serious and raised his right hand to his forehead with a trembling lip while holding back his tears. He knew what was happening, the final earthly farewell to Ben. He saluted Sergeant Benjamin Bailey. Ben released his salute and seemed to receive a renewed energy for just a few seconds as if he was allowed to have a small glimpse of his destination. His piercing blue eyes became clear and he began to smile. For just a tiny moment he was just like the younger Ben when Christopher first shook his hand upon their first meeting that faithful day on the porch. Ben looked squarely into Christopher's eyes. Then with a final burst of almost supernatural energy, he said in a clear strong voice. "Carry on Marine; SEMPER FI."

Ben's eyes gently closed for the last time on this earth and he was welcomed into heaven for a glorious reunion. Christopher stood there for a few more moments with memories and warm feelings of his best friend flooding his mind with all the adventures they had shared the last fifteen years. The man that had so gallantly saved his life was now gone from this earth so quickly he could not believe it. Christopher walked to the foot of Ben's bed and saluted Benjamin Bailey one more time.

"Goodbye Mr. Ben; I love you too; SEMPER FI." He whispered.

Christopher then offered a short prayer. "Thank you Lord for letting me be here to say good bye to one of the greatest men I have ever had the honor to know." Christopher respectfully left Ben's room and straightway ran into Misty who was already headed that way.

"Misty, he's gone.

"Misty grabbed Christopher and hugged him as she began to cry.

"Will you go home with me to tell my parents?" He asked.

"Yes my love, let me brief the staff and I will be right by your side." Misty answered.

Although it was early in the morning Paul and Angela were still up as they feared it was Ben's final hours that day and were already preparing to go to the hospital. When Christopher and Misty told them the sad news Angela sat down and buried her head in her hands and sobbed. After making sure Angela was ok, Paul walked out on the porch. It was a full harvest moon that night with moonbeams reflecting off of the mountains and still waters, one of the most beautiful nights Paul had ever seen. He had been dreading this news for a long time; he had known it was coming and had barely slept since Ben became ill. It was a very similar feeling to when his father had passed. For some unknown reason even to him, Paul was not able to cry about the news. He stored his emotions away for the time being as he still had unsettled feelings in his soul he could not explain. Christopher stood inside the house at the screen door and watched his father. He was worried about him, especially now. He quietly eased out on to the porch and sat down near Paul.

"Dad, are you going to be ok?" He asked.

Paul lifted up his head from his hands to reply. "Yes Son, I'll be fine, how are you handling it?"

"I'm still in kind of a daze, it's hard to believe we won't be seeing Mr. Ben anymore, talking and laughing at his stories; just having him around was a pleasure." Christopher replied.

Paul leaned back in the old rocking chair and stared at the moon while speaking "I was just thinking about a encouraging Bible verse my father told me to remember whenever I would get upset about a friend or loved one passing. "JOHN 14." He said it helped him get through some tough times, especially during the war. Your Grandfather and Ben were the last of what is quickly becoming a disappearing generation of heroes; they had many rough times but they made it through them all relying on their faith and families. It seems the older I get the more I realize just how wise and brave they were. When your Grandfather passed I guess I started clinging to Ben. There were times when I would hang on every word he said and I think I have written down over two hundred stories he told me about the war and your Grandfather. I am really going to miss him. I am just thankful you were there for him son, in his last moments on earth." Paul said.

Christopher paused for a moment. "Dad, Mr. Ben had a message for all of us before he passed."

Christopher told his father about Ben's last message to the family. Paul sat quietly and listened to every detail.

"You know Dad, this might sound strange but I think Mr. Ben was trying to hold on until he heard about Misty and me getting married." Christopher said.

Paul gave a small, almost silent chuckle while nodding his head in agreement.

"No son, that doesn't sound strange at all; that sounds like something Benjamin Bailey would do; he always put other people's needs and happiness before his." Paul answered.

No words were spoken for a few seconds between father and son. For a solemn moment Paul's mind digressed to one of those Saturday mornings just a few years ago when he and Christopher had spent the morning together treasure hunting and the two would always have their riding home talk. Paul looked over at his son. No longer was he a ten year old curious little boy; he was a grown man now. Paul was thankful he would still come and talk to him.

"Thank you for checking on me Son. You have no idea how I appreciate it." Paul said.

"No problem Dad. I just wanted to make sure you were ok." Christopher replied. Christopher was quiet for a few moments then questioned Paul.

"Dad, why does it not get easier to miss the people that have passed away, even after so many years; I mean, I still miss Grandad and Grandma just as if they had left us yesterday?"

Paul hesitated and rubbed his brow sternly with his fingertips for a few seconds before speaking.

"Well Son, I personally believe it is because of their character they had in life, and simply, the unselfish love they offered to not only their families, but everyone. People like that leave us too many great memories for us to ever forget them; it's good that you still keep their memories fresh in your heart, these are qualities you can some day pass down to your future children. Sometimes it makes everyday problems easier to cope with by remembering a funny story or a special phrase they use to repeat often. It's funny, some of the things your Grandad would say are just now making sense to me what he meant." Paul replied shaking his head slightly. "He use to tell me; Paul, no one's spirit will ever die if you keep them alive in your heart."

Christopher rested his right cheek on his half closed fist.

"Wow Dad, I came out here thinking I could help you but you ended up helping me more." Paul laughed out loud. "That's just what Father's do Son. You will find that out when you become one." Paul replied.

Father and Son sat on the porch together talking and remembering their good times over the years with Benjamin Bailey until the sun rose to unveil another cloudless fall day.

The Final Goodbye

The news of Ben's death spread quickly through the community. Paul and Angela were receiving many calls from the town folks offering their help and sympathies. Ben's funeral was not your average one. So many people wanted to verbally eulogize Ben that it had created a time problem for Pastor Major. The Pastor came up with an idea for every person that wished, to write down their thoughts and their personal experience with Ben; he would read as many as he could at the service the rest would be recorded in a book fashion that could be viewed by everyone. Pastor Major marveled at the amount of people that came to say a final good-bye to their friend. He knew exactly how they felt as Ben and he had been as close as brothers since the day Ben walked down the aisle and shook his hand for the first time as a new Christian. Ben had had so many questions and would consult with "The Major "as he called him, often since he received his new life.

Pastor Robert Major gave one of the best eulogies that he ever had spoken. He spoke from the heart of someone who knew and loved Ben. Paul spoke also, relaying the story of how Ben had met his wife, the joys and tragedy he had endured and how the people of Summerville helped to restore his faith in God with their unconditional love. When he finished, the whole congregation was not sad but in a humble respectful way left the church with joy and hope as they knew Ben was in a better place where heartache, sadness and pain do not exist. Ben was honored with a full military funeral and Christopher was the Marine that presented Paul and Angela the American flag that covered Ben's coffin.

Ben had asked Paul for only one personal favor the whole time they had known each other and Paul was honored to carry it out. Benjamin Bailey was laid to rest next to the love of his life; Lit'l O, and his only son Christopher Bennett Bailey.

At the reading of his will, Ben's wishes were for Paul and Walton Griffin to head the secret club and Christopher and Misty to watch over the Veterans Ranch with business as usual. Walton Griffin handed out a separate personal hand written sealed letter to each of the Taylor family members that Ben had left for them. Ben also left Paul the book of stories he had given Lit'l-O so many years ago. Paul found a special home for the book at the Veterans Ranch along with the story of their meeting in which all visitors had access to read. The next few months were hard for just about everyone that was close to Ben, especially around the holiday season. The sleigh rides, the special chocolate chip cookies and all of the special loving tasks Ben would take care of for his elderly neighbors and friends were sadly missed as was his hearty laugh and his love of life with tales of personal experiences only he could relay, always paired with his smile and that twinkle in his eye.

Yes, Benjamin Bailey managed to etch the everlasting mark of a true friend and a loving servant in the heart of every soul he ever met, never asking for anything in return, only asking how he could serve. Only a few would ever know all of the loving things Ben accomplished to help his neighbors and town. Still everyone that knew him would always keep a warm chamber of happy memories in their heart for Benjamin Bailey.

Traveler

*I*t was the first winter snow after Ben's death. Paul made his way to the barn to feed Traveler. When he opened the barn door he saw that Traveler had backed himself up to the old sleigh seemingly asking to be hitched up for a pull. Paul chuckled to himself and said out load.

"The weatherman's got nothing on you ole boy you can smell the snow even before it falls, tell you what, I will hitch you up today and we will........

Paul stopped in mid-sentence. When he came closer to Traveler, his heart fell. The beautiful old steed had bowed down on his knees with his large nostrils touching the ground. Traveler had died. The veterinarian's diagnosis was his heart had given out, but Paul knew better; Traveler had died of a broken heart. Traveler lived to be forty three years old.

Catching Up With Things

*P*aul and his family had been left with quite a few missions that had to be taken care of and it kept them busy just attempting to complete Ben's last wishes. Christopher was near the end of his tour of duty now and he and Misty were planning their wedding. He still was able to take a vital part in helping with the Veteran's Ranch. Since he was a Marine he could identify with many of the men that came there to get back on their feet. It was hard work and time consuming but on the other hand it was very rewarding to see how their stay there was helping the guys.

Paul was trying to keep up with Ben's ranch as well as his own while teaching the temporary tenants on how to farm and take care of the stock. He had made a decision to retire as early as he could to have more time for his chores. Paul also had a few others things he was working on and was anxious to accomplish. Over the years he had written down many stories of Ben's and his father's experiences as soldiers. They had also helped him with information and little known details on the thirteen boys that never made it home from the war. That particular story had haunted Paul since his father and Ben had told him the stories of their bravery. Paul had decided to put the stories in book form to help preserve a piece of history. He had been working on the research off and on for years now since he had first met Ben. He felt that the time was right to put it together as soon as he could.After running the idea passed Cousin Walton, who had some friends who had other friends that knew some very good publishers, Paul proceeded with full steam ahead and finished the book. He called it "THE FINAL SALUTE." Surprisingly to Paul, three publishers contacted him offering him a contract. Paul selected the best one and closed the deal. He decided to give the books out for free to anyone interested. If they wanted they could make a donation to the BEN BAILEY VETERANS RANCH. Paul was very pleased at the kind letters and donations that came in but he was even happier that through this book their stories of bravery and patriotism could be handed down from generation to generation. His greatest honor was when he would receive a visit from many of the true heroes surviving family members. They would make a special trip just to meet and thank him for his research while telling Paul their memories of their relative's life. Paul would always return their kindness with humble thanks of his own for their relatives, ultimate sacrifice for Freedom and Liberty.

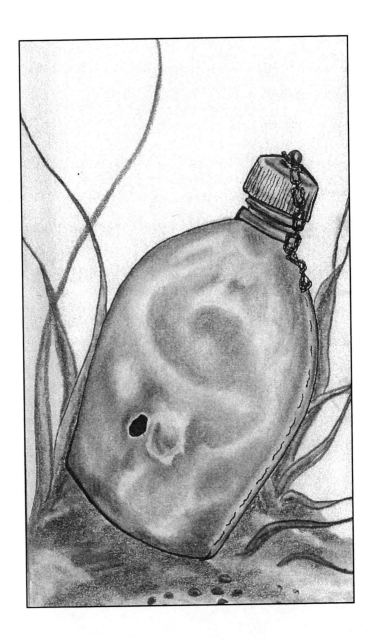

The Monument

Even after life had basically returned to the daily normal routine, Paul still had a daunting restless soul. It was a beautiful late afternoon when he got the notion to just take a walk and try to relax. Angela was still working at the Library so Paul would be walking alone today. Talking to himself he concluded a nice walk would help clear his mind of all of the sadness and loss of the last few months. Before he knew it he was at the foot of Memorial Hill. Paul paused and suddenly realized, in his whole life he had never climbed the hill, why, he did not know. Thinking there is no better time like the present he began to trek up a small winding all but hidden path that eventually ended up at the very top of the beautiful terrain. When he reached his destination Paul turned and looked at his quaint little hometown in the valley. He could see his own home in the distance and the towns dimming lights of the businesses starting to close down for the day. On the other side of the hill were the farmlands and majestic mountains in the background. As the evening air grew heavier the smells of countryside were more acute to his senses. This was truly a special place. It was one of the most peaceful places he had ever been. Paul rested on the hill for a while then decided to return home. Being a treasure hunter most of his years he had a habit of looking down at the ground on most of his walks. Over the years it had rewarded him with many fine arrowheads and old objects left behind from an ancient population.

As he began his journey down the hill, Paul noticed a semi shiny object poking out of the loose red dirt. He bent over and proceeded to gently brush the dirt away from a medium size, what appeared to be a container of some sorts. When Paul separated the object from the earth it did not take him long to realize what he had found. The container had a spout and a hole that was ripped right in the center of it. Could this be? Paul raised the object up to his right ear and gave it a slight shake. After a couple of shakes he heard an object in the container become loose which started to rattle as it struck against its inner walls. Paul had discovered Ben Bailey's old army canteen; the very same canteen that had saved him from taking a bullet from the enemy, and probably saved his life. The same canteen that Ben and Paul's father had buried that faithful night in order to not be discovered planting flower seeds. At that moment this discovery triggered something miraculous and unexplainable in Paul Taylor's soul. It felt like the emotional floodgates that he had been holding back for so many years had broken and washed directly into his sad, grieving heart. His mind flashed back to the day he and his father had taken that life changing horseback ride and the story he had shared to help him.

"All things happen for a reason, Son." Those words were pounding in his brain. Paul helplessly fell to his knees and wept uncontrollably like he had never wept in his life. The only words he was able to speak were "Lord please help me, please give me peace."

At that moment all of his sadness and anxieties of the past flashed before him, purging themselves from his mind and heart. Images and memories of all of his loved ones that had passed from this life that he missed so much were rolling over and over in his mind. Then a gentle and serine peace entered his heart as the earth quickly absorbed his tears. He was now able to say good bye to them. Time seemed to stand still; just for a wonderful supernatural moment.

Paul regained his composure and placed the canteen exactly where he had found it; gently pulled the dirt back over it and buried it for the final time. He slowly rose from his kneeling position and stood straight; realizing God had answered his prayer that evening. He was even free of his lifelong guilt of his many shortcomings, the guilt of ruining the chance to serve his country and the burden of mistakes he had made. Paul's soul was renewed. His heart was cleansed. A Bible verse gently entered his heart and mind. *"I will never leave thee nor forsake thee."* Paul was forgiven and his heart was filled with Joy. His walk home that evening was much different than his journey there. He did a lot of soul searching the next few days and became completely focused on the next mission he needed to accomplish.

A few weeks later the town gave Paul permission to commission the local monument company to create a monument of remembrance for all of the veterans that made the ultimate sacrifice for America. Paul was glad to handle the project and it was not long before the beautiful giant marble monument was placed directly on top of Benjamin Bailey's canteen; the perfect location as it could be beheld from any angle. The monument was made of marble but sculpted to look like wood with a nail spike fused into each end of the arms and one at the foot. It seemed to bring a feeling of pride and peace and more important remembrance to everyone that gazed upon it; but it had a special double meaning to Paul Taylor. At the foot of the monument was a bronze plaque with the names of the thirteen soldiers of the county who never returned from the battlefield. There was also a comforting Bible verse at the bottom of the plaque that read.

"LO, I AM WITH YOU ALWAYS; EVEN TO THE END OF THE EARTH."

Life Goes On

*T*he cycle of life would continue in the little town just as it had always done. It was strange and often bitter-sweet in many ways. Changes in life come to everyone, but the people of Summerville seemed to embrace whatever destiny would be set before them whether good or bad. In the years that followed the process of ageing was pleasant for some and hard to accept for others. It seemed like every year the annual family reunions would be short yet another loved one that had closed their eyes for their final sleep on this earth. They would be remembered in old picture albums or an old story or two told to the next generation that would assume their family responsibilities as they created their own legacies. They would never be forgotten. From time to time, the restless hearts of many of the young would cause them to leave the town to pursue their dreams, but most of them would return years later with a new appreciation of the peaceful life they had left in their home town. All were always welcomed back with open arms and loving hearts.

Monte and Sam would both take over their family businesses carrying on the tradition of vegetable gardening and horse ranching. Many times when the day was slowing down to evening time, Christopher would notice his two boyhood friends sitting up in the tree house probably reminiscing over some long passed childhood memory or adventure. Sometimes he would stop and climb the up the old latter and join them. The three bicycles propped up against the giant oak's trunk were now replaced with pick-up trucks parked in the meadow. As he would listen to the past stories he had heard so many times before, Christopher would sometimes detect a note of sadness in their voices that seemed to long for the life that had passed by them so quickly. Both men seemed to still be searching for their purpose in life.

Pastor Robert Major decided to cash in his honorary members gold coin awarded to him by Benjamin Bailey. He felt led to use the money to start a mission's program based out of the little country church. One Sunday after preaching about the many needs of the mission field, Brother Major ended his sermon by quoting one of his favorite phrases. "Give a man a fish and he will eat for a day; teach a man how to fish and he will eat for a lifetime." He then gave his weekly invitation. At the end of the sermon two figures boldly stepped out of the pews to make their way down the aisle to accept the challenge and dedicate their lives to the Lord. The two men ultimately became two of the greatest missionaries in history and spent the rest of their lives teaching needy countries how to grow food and farm more efficiently, not to mention becoming spiritual "fishers of men."Those two saved souls were Monte and Sam. They had finally found their calling in life.

Arielle Taylor finished medical school and was offered a partnership with Misty Taylor. The two opened up an office very near town that served the community quite well. Arielle specialized in Internal Medicine and was glad to be back close to her family. Paul and Angela were happy she was near. Both Arielle and Misty were inducted in the secret club, which opened up a new pipeline for needy people in town. Their first love would always be looking after the veterans at Benjamin Bailey's Veterans Ranch. They're partnership worked out quite well. As the news of the success of the Bailey Veterans Ranch spread, many physicians would visit just to study the plan of the Ranch and just why it was so successful. On one of these visits Arielle met a young doctor, Captain Jonathan Sharp, still serving in the Navy. The two fell in love and were married a year later. This partnership also worked out very well.

Alyssa Taylor had finished law school and had become a partner in a successful law office in a big city far from Summerville. When Cousin Walton Griffin decided to retire he offered to help Alyssa come back home and start her own practice taking over his clients. And that is exactly what she did. Needless to say Paul and Angela were even happier now that the whole family was near. Walton then was satisfied to become a full time newspaper owner and editor for his town, occasionally assisting Alyssa with some insightful legal advice. Alyssa would also become a great asset to the Bailey Veteran's Ranch assisting the soldiers in legal matters. Alyssa married her high school sweetheart, Landon Connors, who was now the Principal and a coach at Summerville High School. She too was inducted into the secret club and over the years was able to help many a troubled soldier find the road to a happy life.

After a short illness, Aunt Evelyn would pass into eternity in her ninety seventh year. Although her flower garden mourned for her personal touch, it still would do it's best to put on a beautiful show every spring. On occasions Paul would pass by her home place and notice his Cousin Walton walking through her garden or resting under a shade tree in the old swing. Although often tempted to stop, Paul would just wave to his cousin and respect his private time as he remembered his beloved Aunt Evelyn.

Cousin Joyce would take over the operation of the General store. About a year before Aunt Evelyn passed, Mother and daughter decided to cash in both of their gold coins to buy extra food and dry goods if hard times would strike any local residents. When those times inevitably came, Joyce would secretly add an extra dozen eggs and other extra groceries and tidbits here and there to the list without the recipients noticing. She especially received a special personal reward when the down and out party would come in to pay their bill they were struggling with, and, for some strange and unexplainable reason she could not find it. As the customer would leave the store, scratching his head in confusion, Cousin Joyce would just smile and remember her mother.

Paul's old friend Mark Corrigan showed up one day to go fishing with Paul. By the time they had returned home, Mark had decided to sell his shop in the city and move to his favorite place in the world to retire. In the years to follow, Paul would joke about their fishing trip recalling how Mark did not catch a thing; however, Paul said he made the biggest catch of his life convincing Mark to move to Summerville. Mark was never one to sit around and waste a day and quickly found out he was not retirement material, so he offered to buy Angela's shop. It was perfect timing as Angela was feeling led to help out more with the Bailey Veterans Ranch with Christopher and Paul. It also allowed Mark to keep up with the contacts he had in his business. He still would handle a private auction when some extra funds were needed from the secret sale of a gold coin. Angela agreed to sell the shop only if Mark would retain Bobi Stone to work there. Mark agreed; he and Bobi Stone hit it off immediately as they had much in common. Bobi Stone would continue to paint beautiful landscapes. Mark and Bobi were married a few years later and spent the rest of their lives in Summerville.

Fil and Mil could no longer stand being separated with such a long distance from their children, grandchildren and now great grandchildren so they decided to move, to the delight of everyone, to Summerville. They immediately became the new welcome citizens of the community. Fil wasted no time fulfilling his life's dream of building his own small sailboat in which he would help many a local teenager earn their "sea legs" teaching them the wonderful art of sailing on the large lake just outside of town. From day one, Fil knew exactly what the boat's name would be. It came from when Christopher was young and he was unable to pronounce "Grandpa." As all young kids do, he made up his own name for his grandpa. Fil promised himself if he were ever able to own a boat he would name it after the endearing nickname his first grandson had bestowed on him. Mil kept busy with her eternal energy and would pass along her special recipes to the local ladies from time to time and was constantly being drafted to organize a new fundraiser or charity event. The couple would enjoy their new life and their new home for many years to come. They were even voted the town's official great grandparents and lived up to the title handsomely. They also loved to travel, however, both would always comment on how it was so good to be back home. They would enjoy their retirement years and most of the time you would find them sailing and laughing, enjoying the day together, on the S.S. FRAMPA.

Christopher made it through his tour of duty and came home safely from the Marine Corps. He wasted no time in taking over the duties of a cattle rancher. After he and Misty married they offered to purchase Paul's parents home. Paul and Angela were thrilled for them to move there and around two years later Christopher and Misty had a baby boy making Paul and Angela proud grandparents. They named their son James Paul Benjamin Taylor.

Christopher wanted his name to include the three men in his life that he considered his heroes. Paul would often joke about the length of his grandson's name. He would say; "Now if Ben Bailey were here he would say." "That is the only child I have ever seen where you could start saying his name at breakfast time and just be finishing up saying it by suppertime." But they all agreed Ben would probably spoil his little namesake without remorse.

Misty's father became very ill. One day during a father daughter talk, Misty tearfully told her father the whole story of who was responsible for the money that saved their farm so many years ago. Her frail father took her hand and told her.

"Misty my love; soon I am going to be able to thank Ben Bailey in person." A few days later he made good on his promise.

The Benjamin Bailey Veterans Ranch continued to operate successfully thanks to all of the town's volunteers. Sergeant Bailey's army picture had been added on the old walnut wall next to his son's and his best friend. Under the pictures and a large banner reading "Semper Fi" was a table with copies of Paul's book, "The Final Salute" free for the taking. In the years to follow the Veterans Ranch would continue to be successful in fulfilling the lives of America's bravest which also fulfilled the dream of its founder.

The discovery of the gold coins was never spoken about in mixed company and the secret find of the century would continue to be an expanding everlasting gift to anyone in need in the community for many years to come. By giving the treasure back to the ancestors of the very people his ancestor had stolen from, Benjamin Bailey had done much more than just repay the town back. The secret club would continue to carefully induct many more members as the years passed; all would take their responsibilities very seriously. Benjamin Bailey would have been proud.

Angela would continue to write the secret instruction letters when needed. With every letter she wrote, her special memories of Benjamin Bailey's kindness and unselfish love for his town would flood her heart. The feeling that this was her special calling in life would sustain a happiness in her heart for the rest of her life. Paul was never able to find out any more unanswered details on the Samuel Bailey stagecoach robbery, but as the years passed he grew to accept that maybe he really did not need to solve all of these mysteries and just enjoy life just as his father had advised him.

Paul was pleased to accept the way things had worked out with the treasure. On most evenings Paul would retire to the front porch and gaze out at the beautiful sunset. He would watch as the sun would slowly set behind Memorial Hill with her new monument creating a gleaming silhouette of hope for mankind and the reminder of ultimate sacrifice while painting a final breathtaking portrait of the day. Paul thought himself a bit silly at times but the hill seemed to be fulfilled now; almost like it was just waiting for someone to reveal its true reason for being created. Sometimes Angela would join her husband just to sit and talk and hold his hand.

Many evenings hardly a word was spoken but they were always joined at their hearts. She was the only person he ever confided in of the discovery of Ben's canteen. He knew she understood the peace he had now. No one on this earth knew him better than his life's partner and no one on this earth loved him more.

After the sun would disappear and the heavy blanket of night would safely secure the countryside; Paul and Angela would retire for the night. Still holding hands, they would enter the now empty house where so many warm memories would cheerfully haunt them; then drift off to sleep with a peace in their hearts and a prayer of thanksgiving on their lips for another day and all of their blessings. Both now looked forward to the weekly Sunday lunch gathering of the whole Taylor family that Angela had skillfully turned into a weekly tradition.

As the people of Summerville all retired for the night, the ole No.2 train would pass through the town on its last run and blow it's good night whistle signaling the end of another day.

For as long as he lived and with every grandchild that would follow, Paul Taylor would do his best to become a living witness of the good parts of life as well as a comforter to the tragic. It was not uncommon to see him with his trusty metal detector on top of a hill or at an old home site abandoned years before, teaching a little one the rules of do's and don'ts and the proper etiquette of digging up things that were long abandoned and forgotten. Most of the time it would become a history lesson; and you can be sure Paul Taylor never missed a chance to pass on some real treasure stories; and he would always be sure to include those special stories of those "True Treasures "of his little hometown of Summerville and the Loving Lord that kept watch over them all.

Beep…Beep…Beep… BEEEEEEEP..

"Hey Dad Hey Grand Dad. Whatcha think it is?"

THE END

About The Author

*P*erry T. Montague grew up on a farm in Tennessee. His love of history and small towns helped him discover the fascinating sport of metal detecting. As his family grew, with obligations to work, daily chores, plus moving to a larger city, he was unable to pursue his hobby as much as he would like, so he decided to write a book incorporating colorful characters along with an exciting treasure hunt. Yes, Perry does get to pull out his detector and blow the dust off of it and sweep over a few forgotten fields from time to time, however, writing this story was even more satisfying. It is his hope that The Treasures of Summerville will be enjoyed by people of all ages and parents will feel good about reading it to their children.